Iron Age Promontory Forts in the Northern Isles

R. G. Lamb

BAR British Series 79
1980

B.A.R.

B.A.R., 122 Banbury Road, Oxford OX2 7BP, England

GENERAL EDITORS

A. R. Hands, B.Sc., M.A., D.Phil.
D. R. Walker, M.A.

B.A.R. 79, 1980: "Iron Age Promontory Forts in the Northern Isles".
©R. G. Lamb, 1980.

The author's moral rights under the 1988 UK Copyright,
Designs and Patents Act are hereby expressly asserted.

All rights reserved. No part of this work may be copied, reproduced, stored, sold, distributed, scanned, saved in any form of digital format or transmitted in any form digitally, without the written permission of the Publisher.

ISBN 9780860540878 paperback
ISBN 9781407323510 e-book
DOI https://doi.org/10.30861/9780860540878
A catalogue record for this book is available from the British Library
This book is available at www.barpublishing.com

CONTENTS

		Page
I	Brochs and Cliff-Castles	1
II	The Shetland Blockhouses and their Relations	11
III	The Multivallate Forts and the Western Seaways	43
IV	The Meaning of Forts and Brochs	65

Appendices

1	Gazetteer	71
2	Nesnám	88
3	Promontory-sited Castles	90
Bibliography		97
Index		100
Plates		103

LIST OF ILLUSTRATIONS

Figure		Page
1	British Isles, promontory-fort coasts	5
2	Orkney, places mentioned in the text	8
3	Shetland, places mentioned in the text	9
4	Loch of Huxter and Ness of Burgi blockhouse forts	10
5	Clickhimin site plain	14
6	Broch of Nybster, RCAMS plan	21
7	Brough of Bigging, Orkney	22
8	Sgarbach, Caithness	23
9	Dun Mhairtein, Sutherland	24
10	Burgi Geos, Shetland	28
11	Burgi Geos, 1853 sketch	30
12	Scatness North Fort, Shetland	32
13	Taing of Brough, Unst, Shetland	36
14	The Landberg, Fair Isle	44
15	Hog Island Sound, Shetland	45
16	Profiles of Brough Ness of Garth, The Landberg and Hog Island Sound	46
17	Brough of Stoal, Shetland	48
18	Brough of Qindwick, Orkney	49
19	Brough of Borgastoon, Shetland	51
20	Burland, Shetland; Onstan, Orkney; Burwick, Orkney; RCAMS plans	52
21	Doon Eask, Co Kerry	55
22	Cahercarberymore, Co Kerry	56
23	Cornish cliff-castles, Kenidjack Castle and Giants Castle	57
24	Houbie and Snabroch, Shetland, RCAMS plans	63
25	Castle of Sand Geo, Orkney	67
26	Castle of Old Wick, Caithness	91
27	Lilleborg, Bornholm	93
28	Lambhoga Head, Dunrossness, Shetland	95

LIST OF PLATES

Plate		Page
1	Ness of Burgi	103
2	Clickhimin blockhouse	103
3	Loch of Huxter	103
4	Dun Mhairtein	104
5	Dun Mhairtein, rampart	104
6	Burgi Geos	105
7	Burgi Geos, the approach	105
8	Burgi Geos, chevaux-de-frise	106
9	Burgi Geos, the cliff	106
10	Burgi Geos, blockhouse	107
11	Burgi Geos, ringwall	107
12	Scatness North Fort	108
13	Scatness North Fort, wall-face	108
14	The Landberg	109
15	The Landberg, horseshoe bank	109
16	The Landberg, outer banks	110
17	Hog Island Sound	110
18	Brough of Stoal	111
19	Brough of Stoal, rampart	111
20	Castle of Sand Geo	111
21	Brough Ness of Garth	112
22	Brough Ness of Garth, wall	112
23	Castle of Old Wick	113
24	Castle of Old Wick, great tower	113
25	Borve Castle	114
26	Castle of Brough	114

PREFACE

This study is based on field surveys made between 1970 and 1973. The first two of those years in particular were memorable summers—the sun shone, and Shetland was still the old Shetland, when there were steamers not ro-ro ferries, and fishing boats in Lerwick harbour, and motorists who drove crazily but never, ever hit the sheep, and Sullom Voe had not been heard of outside the islands. A. O. Curle, who single-handedly did the early Royal Commission surveys in Sutherland and Caithness, in the high summer of the Edwardian era, would have found it a not unfamiliar world; and I cannot claim that my methods were any advance on his. By 1973 it all was changing very fast, and while the Shetland landscape continues to offer unique opportunities for original archaeological research based on surface fieldwork, I fear that future students there will have to search much harder for the Shetland that I was privileged to experience.

The work was done for my PhD thesis at Birmingham University where it was presented in 1973. The cost was met by a Major State Studentship from the Department of Education and Science, and additional grants for the purchase of equipment were received from the Marion Ruth Courtauld Fund, Braintree. The subject originally was suggested by Mr. P. S. Gelling and the work was sustained by his help, encouragement and amused tolerance. As it turned out however the thesis was largely devoted to eremitic monasteries, which I came across by accident while looking for promontory forts, and this subject I subsequently was able to pursue on a research fellowship at the University of Newcastle-upon-Tyne. The monastic part of my thesis has become very out-of-date and no-one now ought to read it, but my ideas on the forts have not greatly changed. Little more, I think, can be done with them by surface fieldwork, and the next stage will have to be excavation. I am not an enthusiastic excavator (although to dig Burgi Geos would be fun) and hope that this will be done by others. In the meantime I have tried to avoid producing the sort of publication which is too obviously an undigested PhD thesis (PSG's words) and have re-written the text.

I must especially thank the Royal Commission on Ancient Monuments (Scotland) for their readily-given permission to use their own site plans, which appear as Figs, 4, 6, 20 and 24; and the General Editors of B.A.R. for their patience with my delays.

R. G. Lamb
Kirkwall, March 1980

I

BROCHS AND CLIFF-CASTLES

The brochs, surely the greatest engineering achievement of prehistoric Britain, dominate the Iron Age archaeology of the Northern Isles. The broch of Mousa still stands over 13m high; Culswick, until it was plundered for its stone late in the eighteenth century, nearly matched it. To construct stable walls of such height, in unmortared masonry of undressed stones shaped only by splitting, called for an engineer's understanding of force and stress; how that understanding was developed remains one of the more controversial questions of European prehistory. Mousa, as E. W. MacKie has pointed out, must be the apogee of a long development, and we reasonably can expect there to have been a succession of increasingly elaborate structures representing the refinement of the principles of broch architecture.

The key principle is the hollow or double wall. To build high in this kind of drystone, one has to build broad; but a broad wall of great height is inherently unstable because the small individual stones tend to behave as a fluid when under great pressure. Such a wall is liable to be pushed apart at the base, by the internal stresses set up by its own great weight. The solution is to build two parallel or concentric walls, about a metre apart, each of these walls being much narrower than would be necessary for it to stand alone; the two walls are secured together at intervals by stone-slab ties, and in effect prop each other up. An understanding of stresses is shown too by the series of voids, each spanned by a lintel and diminishing in width with the height of the wall, which relieve the dead weight of stone which otherwise might crack the great lintels spanning the doorway and internal openings.

The brochs are part of what MacKie (1965, 100) has called the "small stone fort complex" of the Scottish Iron Age in the Highlands and Islands. There is a multiplicity of these small forts, variants on the theme of an enclosure defended by a stout drystone wall. On the Ordnance Survey's period map of Southern Britain in the Iron Age, hillforts are classed by size, and the smallest category is three acres (1.2ha.) or under. By comparison, the small stone forts of the Highland region, often only a few hundred square metres in area, seem very small indeed. This reflects the difficulty of communications and the small and localised quality of communities; no fort in the Highlands or Islands presumably could command so great a population as one of the great Wessex hillforts. In terms of area enclosed, the brochs are the smallest of all these forts (although in Shetland in particular, they often lie at the heart of larger complexes of defensive outworks), but the most spectacular and ambitious in execution.

The hollow-wall technique is peculiar to the brochs and to some of their near relatives, the galleried duns and the blockhouses. The basic art of drystone-building itself is common to all the forts and is immeasurably ancient. Some of the architectural details of brochs also are shared with the small drystone forts. In particular, the characteristic broch entrance passage, in two sections—a narrower outer followed by a wider inner, with the door-position between the two marked by slab-checks and mural barholes—is found throughout the small stone fort complex.

Brochs first seriously came to the attention of the scholarly world when in 1777 John Williams published his account of "remarkable ancient ruins lately discovered in the Highlands and northern parts of Scotland", chiefly featuring Dun Dornaig (Dun Dornadilla) in Strathmore. Mousa was remarked upon and sketched by some of the early tourists, but the first thorough account was that of Dryden in 1857. The clearing-out of brochs then became a gentlemanly pursuit, many of those now open to view having been freed of their debris in the second half of the nineteenth century. This period saw a lengthy controversy on the date of the monuments, for excavators were particularly struck by the extreme scarcity or absence of metal objects among the finds. The respected northern scholar and translator of the "Heimskringla", Samuel Laing, was the leading proponent of a Stone Age date, while Fergusson, discovering that broch distribution coincided with areas of Norse settlement, argued for a Scandinavian origin. The careful work of Joseph Anderson eventually established their Iron Age context.

None of these early excavations even approximated to modern stratigraphic methods, although the quantities of finds—pottery and stone artefacts—were impressive. Serious difficulties arise from this situation—although we often see references to "broch pottery" no Northern broch yet has produced pottery definitely associated with the construction and immediate use of the broch, rather than with the inevitable secondary occupation with wheelhouses or slab-structures. The dangers of this situation were cogently presented in an important paper by R. B. K. Stevenson in 1955. But even two major excavations done on Orkney brochs in the 1930s, at Midhowe (Callander and Grant 1934) and Gurness, which is still unpublished, did very little to put the brochs into an historical context, and threw no light on their origins and development.

There were two apparent lines of relationship from the brochs. One was to the rest of the small stone fort complex, particularly to the galleried duns of the western seaboard; the other was to the circular, massively-built houses with radial piers to support the roof, known as wheelhouses. Wheelhouses were found closely associated with brochs, as well as independently; some brochs, including Mousa, had wheelhouses erected inside them as a form of secondary occupation. These circular buildings seemed to be part of a general Iron Age roundhouse tradition of which Little Woodbury was established as the type-site in the timber-building regions, and which was found in the stone-using south-west of Britain at such sites as Chysauster and Chun Castle. Since brochs too could be considered a form of roundhouse, it was possible to see them as domestic rather than military, whereas the association with the "small stone fort complex" would favour an origin within a fort-building tradition.

The real groundwork of modern broch studies was done by Sir Lindsay Scott. He worked primarily in the Hebrides and published his results in two important papers, "The Problem of the Brochs" (1947) and "Gallo-British Colonies" (1948). Scott's method was exemplary, an extensive programme of surface fieldwork followed by intensive study of selected sites by excavation. His eventual conclusion was that the brochs were primarily houses, and that few of them had been of great height (Mousa being exceptional); like the wheelhouses, they derived from a house-building tradition which Scott traced to south-west England. The objections against this view were summarised by Angus Graham in an appendix to the "Problem" paper; but the alternative view, that the brochs were built as forts and were derived from a fort-building tradition, encountered the difficulty that the putative prototype fortifications were not immediately obvious. The western galleried duns did resemble brochs, but it was not agreed whether these were an early type of broch-like fortification, or degenerate brochs devolved in the West from the perfect forms of the North.

The argument had not been settled when J. R. C. Hamilton took in hand the excavation of the enormous Jarlshof site, on the southern extremity of Shetland Mainland. This had been under excavation, on and off, since storm-waves had revealed it at the beginning of the century; it held the promise of an uninterrupted sequence of settlements from earliest times to the late Middle Ages. Hamilton's unravelling of the complicated phases of the Norse houses and middens, was a masterpiece of technique; but for the Early Iron Age— in spite of the presence of a well-preserved broch and several wheelhouses— the site was a disappointment. A sterile layer of clean sand suggested that, between the end of a late Bronze Age settlement and the building of the broch tower, the place had lain abandoned; and the critical centuries during which broch architecture had developed, were not represented in the archaeological record.

The Jarlshof excavation report appeared very promptly in 1956, as Hamilton was beginning work on another Shetland broch. He had chosen Clickhimin, a complex of broch and outworks in a loch on the edge of Lerwick. The site had one particular feature, the curious free-standing "blockhouse", which made it an attractive choice. In a paper read before the Lerwick Viking Congress, W. D. Simpson (1954) had suggested that, contrary to the generally held idea, the Clickhimin blockhouse and ringwall were earlier than the broch. A parallel for the Clickhimin blockhouse is a promontory fort called Ness of Burgi, just across the bay from Jarlshof; perhaps the abandonment of Jarlshof was connected with the building of this fort, in which case the same occupation-context should be represented at Clickhimin. In the event, the excavation was a disappointment; unlike the sand-blown Jarlshof, Clickhimin had shallow deposits and uncertain stratigraphy. Definitive evidence was lacking and the interpretation has aroused controversy. It centres on the social implications claimed by Hamilton (1968) for the Clickhimin structures; he considered that the fortifications and the buildings within and alongside them, reflected an heroic society, and that memories of Clickhimin-type structures were perpetuated in the old Irish prose epics. The idea that this epic material might provide a "window on the Iron Age" was being proposed by Professor K. H. Jackson (1964). Hamilton suggested that this sort of society was established in Shetland by Celtic invaders, who built the blockhouse forts, by the fourth century B.C.

The relationship between brochs and galleried duns meanwhile was receiving the attention of other researchers. There was a strong case for regarding galleried duns as late and degenerate brochs (Young 1962) but E. W. MacKie made a detailed study of duns, brochs and wheelhouses, and reached the opposite conclusion (1965). At Jarlshof, wheelhouses had succeeded the broch, and MacKie established that this was the normal chronological relationship. Of the Hebridean galleried duns, he selected a class which varied between a promontory-fort design and a cliff-edge-positioned D-shaped form, to which he applied the term "semibrochs" (a word coined sixty years earlier by Erskine Beveridge, but used by him less selectively). These MacKie proposed were the prototypes for the brochs. Brochs he saw beginning in this way in the Hebrides, at first being relatively broad and low in shape; as the type spread northward, it was refined to produce a taller and stronger building, reaching its culmination in Shetland. MacKie subsequently was able to show by radiocarbon that the semibrochs could antedate the brochs by perhaps a hundred years.

MacKie's scheme thus has emphasized the Hebrides as the origin centre of broch architecture—although brochs in Shetland, Orkney and Caithness are much more numerous and better built. His 1965 paper minimised the importance of the Shetland blockhouses as having much influence on the brochs. Hamilton's Clickhimin report, although it appeared in print three years later, had been written independently of MacKie's work, and incorporated the same basic assumption of the chronological priority of galleried duns over brochs; the Shetland blockhouse Hamilton saw as a northern relative of the galleried dun.

At every stage, these arguments have been enmeshed in the wider issue, whether an explanation of the broch and allied cultures of the North Atlantic Iron Age, is to be found in diffusionist theory. Professor V. G. Childe (1935 and 1940) drew attention to the parallels in material culture between Atlantic Scotland and South-Western England, and was prepared to state categorically that the south-western origin of the broch culture was a fact of British archaeology. Scott (1948) argued in much more detail for an immigration from the South-West into the Hebrides in the last century B.C., and more recently MacKie (1969b) has proposed an immigration from Wessex in similar circumstances. In the present decade, the validity of all these invasion hypotheses has been challenged by Clarke (1970 and 1971). All were based on the stone roundhouse plans and on certain small items of material culture, such as bone dice. The multivallate promontory forts which are discussed in the third chapter of the present study, have not figured in these arguments, although they provide the most immediate but puzzling of parallels between the northern and southern extremities of Britain's Atlantic seaboard.

*   *   *   *   *

Coastal promontory forts—"cliff-castles"—are among the least understood archaeological field monuments in Britain. Their distribution is almost entirely western, the forts being grouped in Cornwall, Ireland, the Welsh

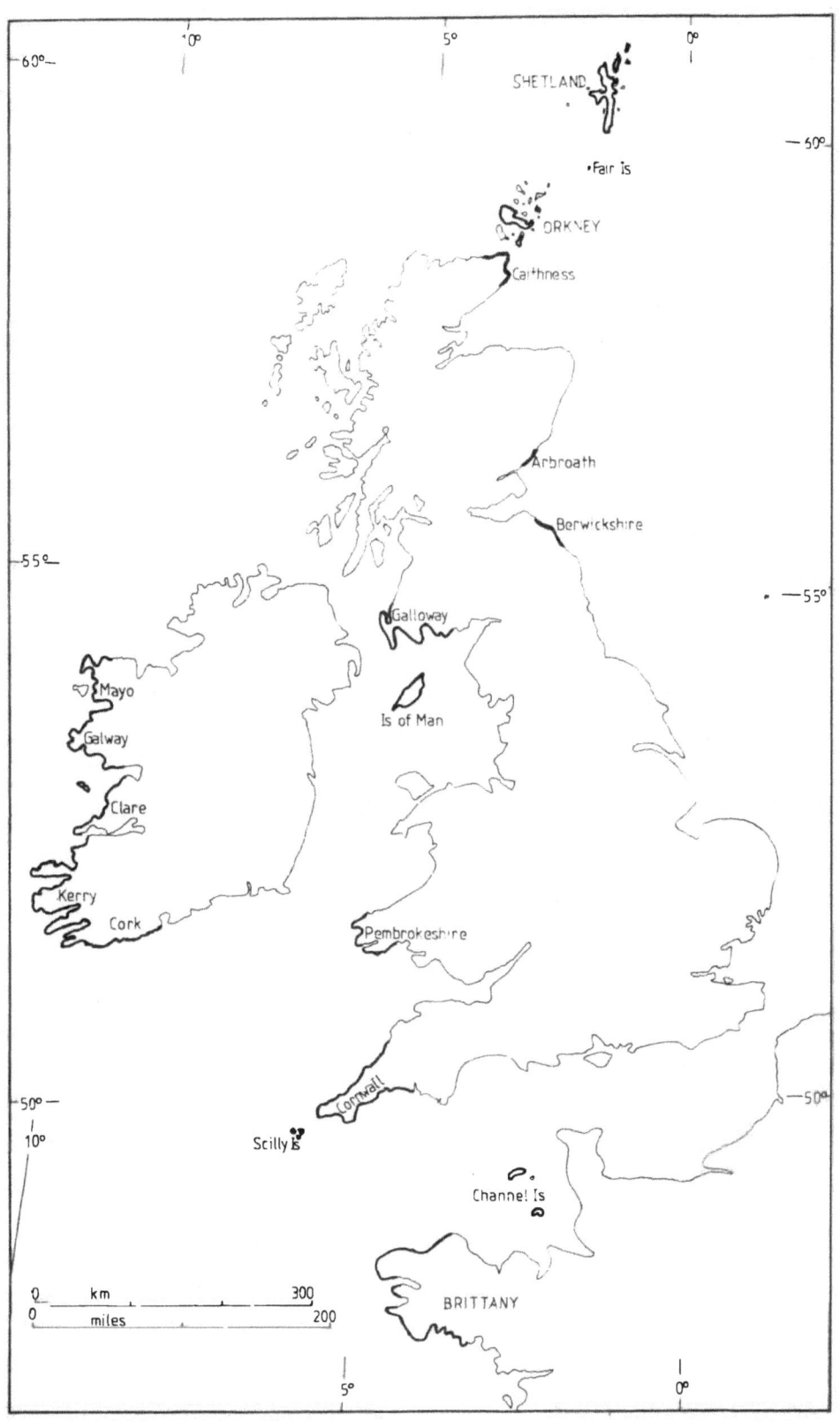

Fig. 1   Britain, Ireland and NW France, with approximate extent of main promontory-fort coasts indicated by heavy outline

coasts, the Isle of Man, and Golloway, and also to the south in Brittany (fig. 1). On the east coast of Great Britain there are two small groups, one in Berwickshire and the other around Arbroath; the forts are entirely absent from the English coast between Dorset and Berwickshire and from most of the eastern coasts of Scotland. Their appearance in the extreme North so far has escaped attention. —This restricted distribution suggests that the promontory forts represent a tradition in themselves and are not just an adaptation of the local brand of hillfort to a coastal site; for the areas deficient in coastal promontory forts are not without inland hillforts. In Orkney and Shetland there are only brochs, broch-related structures, and promontory forts, although the islands have many hills which would have been perfectly suitable for hillforts.

In the southern promontory fort areas, where the existence of the sites always has been known, the state of archaeological knowledge is little better than in the Northern Isles where the sites as a class have gone unrecognized. There is a dearth of excavated evidence; very few forts have been examined—two or three each in Brittany, Cornwall, Ireland and the Isle of Man, none so far in Galloway. Even the excavated examples, usually through no fault of the excavators', seldom have produced evidence of date or of the type of occupation within the fort. Archaeologists starved of facts have made unjustifiable assumptions, such as the link between the cliff-castles of Brittany and Cornwall and the maritime Celtic tribe, the Veneti of Caesar's Gallic War commentaries. This situation offers little hope of fixing the context of the northern forts by direct comparison with the southern ones. Within Orkney and Shetland however, we at least can study the relationship between promontory forts and brochs. The problematical structures called blockhouses, which now are recognized to be a manifestation of pre-broch military architecture, seem to have their origins in promontory forts; and many brochs in Shetland particularly, are sited on promontories within outworks the layout of which reflects a promontory-fort tradition. In the Northern Isles therefore, the study of promontory forts should contribute to our understanding of the background to the broch-building phenomenon, and also pose questions about the occurrence of forts, especially multivallate ones, at both northern and southern extremities of Britain's Atlantic seaboard, with possible implications of culture transmission along the western seaways.

* * * * *

The archaeological usage of the words "broch" and "dun" is the cause of endless confusion, but is too well established to be alterable. Old Norse borg in the dialect of Shetland, Orkney and Caithness becomes a word which rhymes with loch and is variously spelled broch, brough or burgh. It means simply a fortified place or a place strong by artifice or by nature, and as a place-name element can refer to any strong place which may be a built fortress, a natural bastion of the cliffs, or a rock-stack in the sea; many of these places are not forts at all, but eremitic monastic settlements of early mediaeval date. The use of the particular spelling broch as a class-name for the tower-like structures of which Mousa is the archetype, is a modern usage adopted by archaeologists, and is without local authority. The convention has developed, of using the spelling brough when the site is not a broch in the archaeologists' sense. Thus the Broch of Mousa is a broch, while the Brough of Deerness is a peninsular rock with a monastery on it. This has not always been too readily appreciated, and confusion has arisen when archaeologists have tried to find brochs on every site called the Brough of something-or-other. There is a site in the island of Yell which the Royal Commission calls the Broch of Stoal, and is determined must be the site of a broch which has fallen into the sea—in fact, the Brough of Stoal is a very fine example of a multivallate promontory fort which probably never had a broch in it.

There is no distinction in pronunciation between broch and brough, because they are the same word. This causes problems in lecturing and conversation; it is not easy to explain that the Brough of Stoal is not a broch, and that the Broch of Clickhimin strictly should be the Brough of Clickhimin since the name refers to the whole complex of defences and not just to the broch at the heart of it. There is no help for this. In the North, Brough is never, on any account, pronounced Bruff—a pronunciation which belongs to southern places, such as Yorkshire.

In the Gaelic-speaking areas the word is dun which is the broad equivalent of the Norse borg. Thus anything called Brough or Broch in Shetland is a Dun in the Hebrides. Dun is used in a specialist application by archaeologists, to mean a small stone fort, normally a ring-fort. Dun in a Gaelic place-name can of course refer to what archaeologists call a broch, such as Dun Carloway, Dun Telve, and Dun Dornaig. And Dun Mhairtein is a promontory fort which archaeologists would not call a dun, according to their own use of the word.

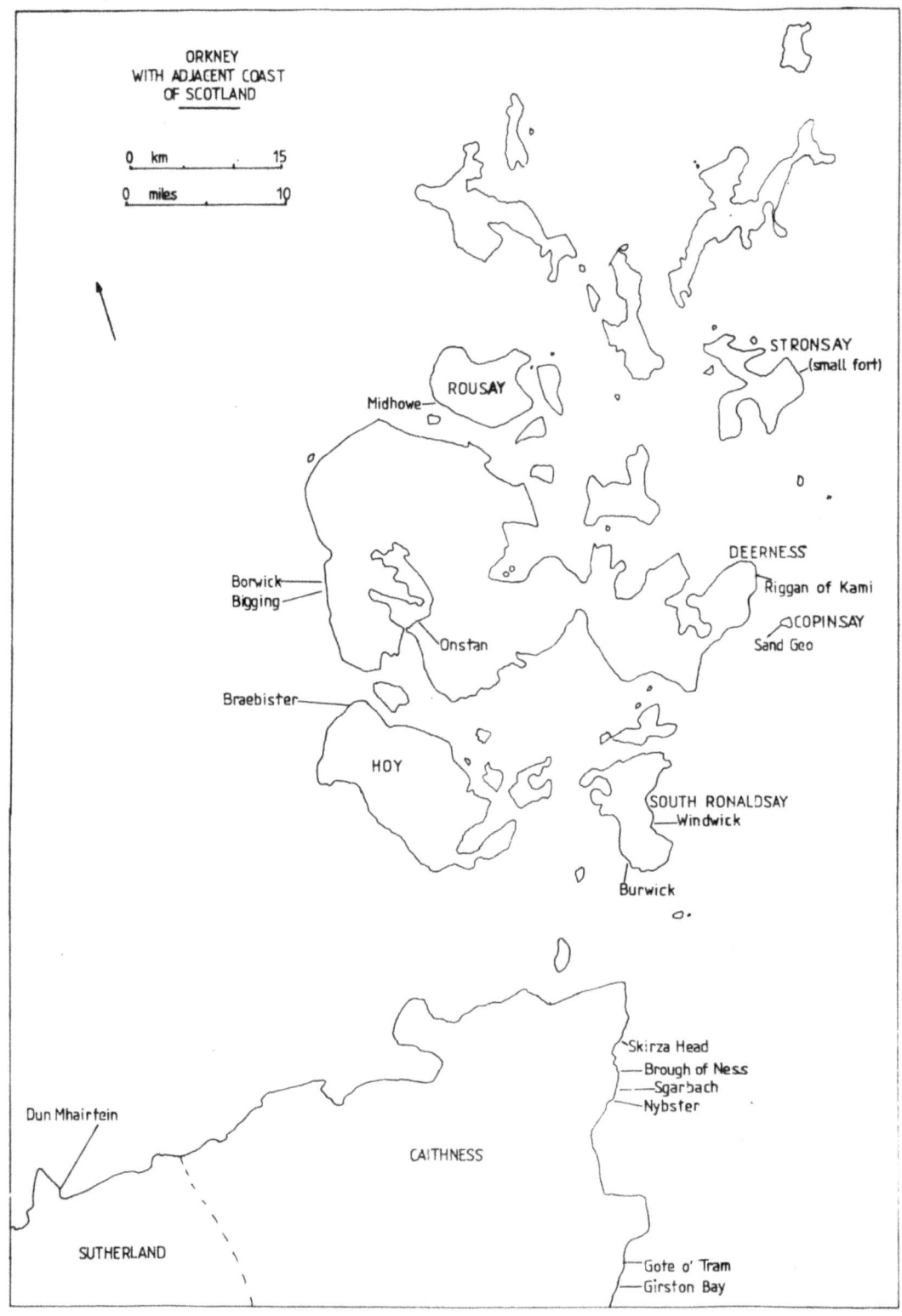

Fig. 2 Orkney and adjacent Scottish coast: places mentioned in the text

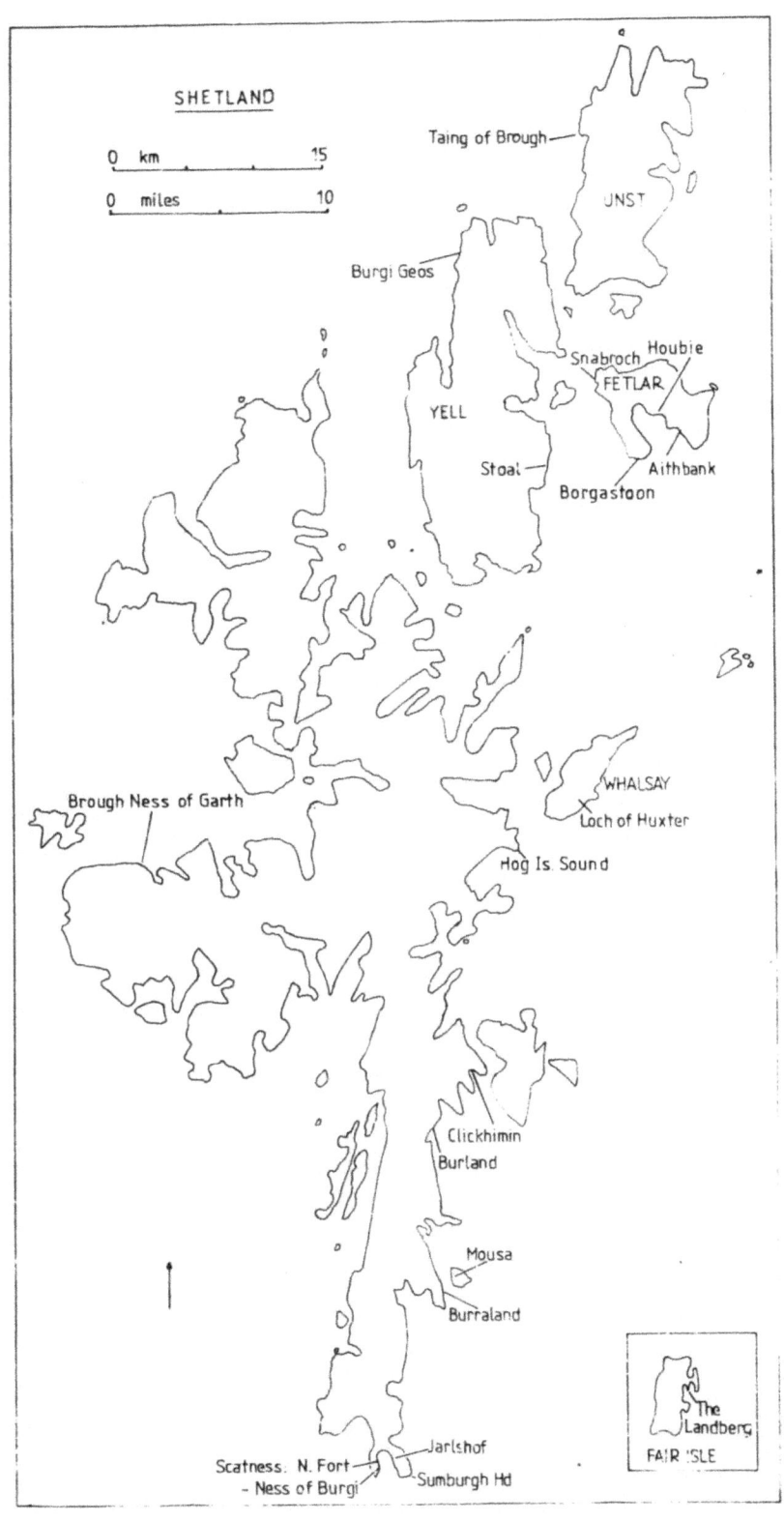

Fig. 3   Shetland: places mentioned in the text

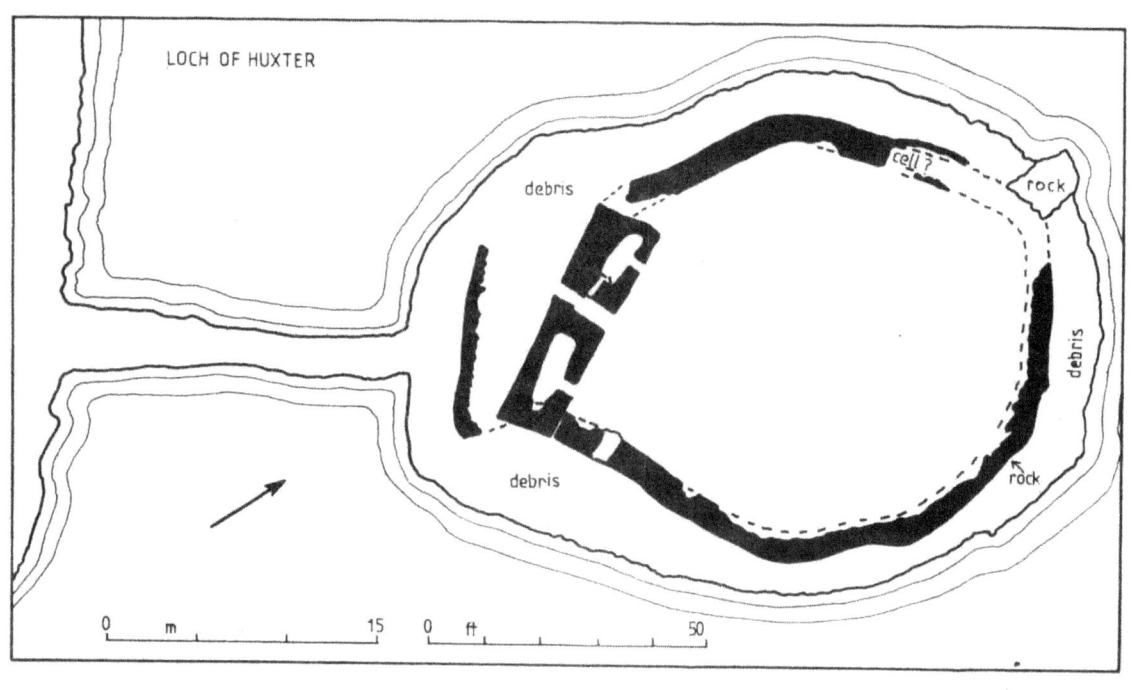

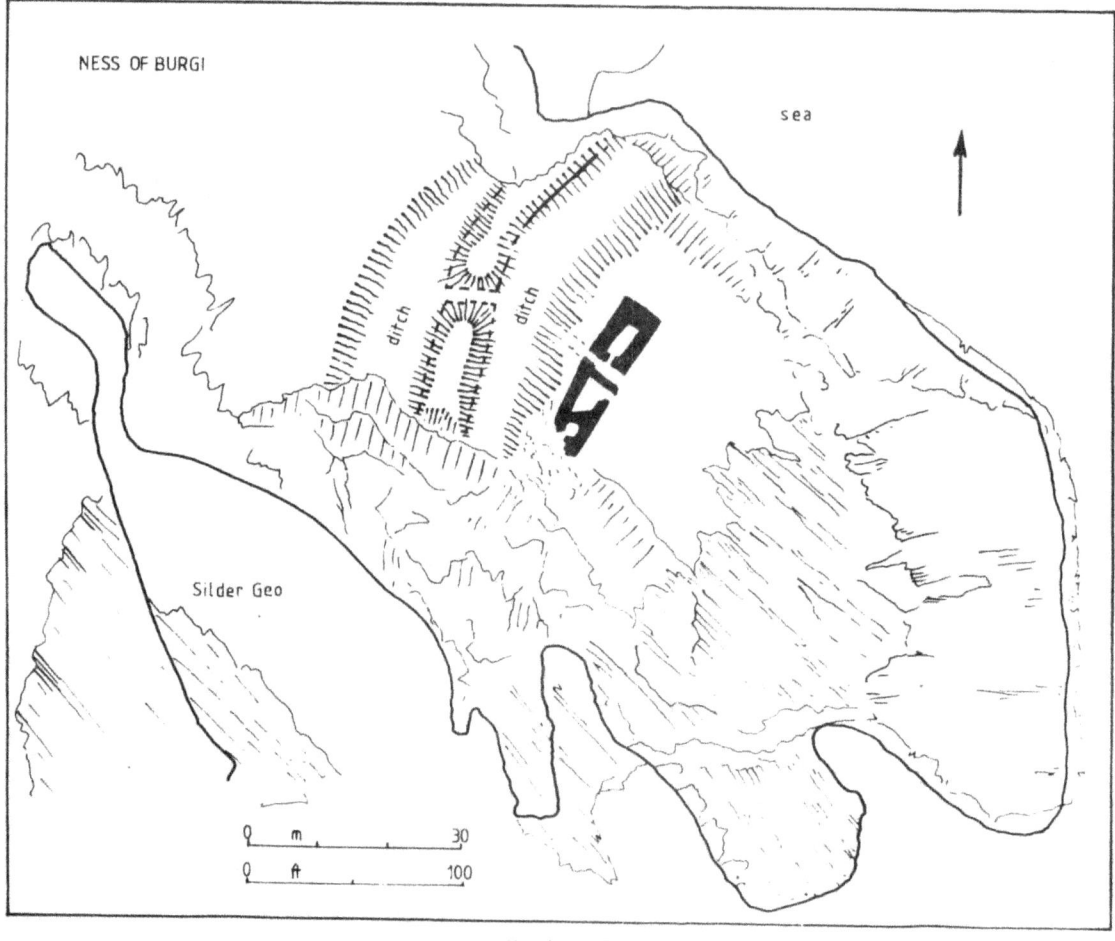

Fig. 4 Shetland blockhouse forts: (above) Loch of Huxter (below) Ness of Burgi

II

THE SHETLAND BLOCKHOUSES AND THEIR RELATIONS

Three structures on widely separated sites in Shetland have for long been acknowledged as forming a peculiar class known as Blockhouse forts—Ness of Burgi, Loch of Huxter, and Clickhimin. Architecturally they have some broch-like characteristics, but their date and function long remained doubtful. The Clickhimin one was exhaustively studied by J. R. C. Hamilton during his excavation campaign in the 1950s, which examined the whole of this broch, blockhouse and ring-fort complex; but the excavations were inconclusive, the relationships among the elements still remaining a matter for conjecture. Hamilton however following some earlier scholars, remarked on the resemblance of the blockhouses to the massive forework constructions on the broch sites of Midhowe and Nybster, thus opening up the possibility that the origins of blockhouses are in some way involved with promontory forts.

The largest of the Shetland blockhouses is on the low and rocky promontory of Scatness, which with the much higher headland of Sumburgh to the east, forms the broad bay known as West Voe of Sumburgh. This southernmost extremity of Sheltand once was its most valuable farming area, but catastrophic sand-blow during the late seventeenth and early eighteenth centuries—an environmental disaster which is not fully understood—reduced most of it to a waste of shifting dunes. This formerly rich area has many prehistoric settlement traces, the most famous of which is the extensive and complex settlement at Jarlshof, on the north-eastern shore of the West Voe. Immediately opposite Jarlshof, on the east-facing side of the Scatness peninsula, is the blockhouse fort of Ness of Burgi (fig. 4).

Scatness although low-lying is hedged with dangerous reefs, and the normal access to Ness of Burgi always must have been overland. As one walks southwards, the promontory narrows and at one point drops nearly to sea level, where the grassed surface gives way to a storm-beach of boulders. After picking one's way across these it is necessary to scramble up a rugged staircase of rock to the southward continuation of the peninsula. Shortly beyond here, the promontory is barred by a low bank. Then Scatness broadens again to an expanse of turf and sea-pink, and from its eastern side projects the subsidiary promontory called Ness of Burgi. The Ness is protected by two rock-cut ditches between which is a stone-revetted rampart, with entrance gap centrally placed. From the bottom of the inner ditch to the summit of the promontory is a sharp slope, at the top of which, behind a narrow berm, stands the blockhouse (pl. 1). Ness of Burgi blockhouse, before restoration in 1971, was over 22.5 m. long and varied between 5.6 m and 6.4 m in width. Through it is an entrance passage in line with the gap in the outer rampart. The passage is of the form common to the other blockhouses which have them, as well as to brochs; a narrower outer section, in this case beginning at

0.9 m and narrowing to 0.7 m at the inner end of the section, where there are two slab doorchecks and a pair of holes in the walls, for drawbars. The inner section of passage is 1.2 m wide immediately behind the door and narrows to 1.1 m where it emerges on the rear of the building. The blockhouse contained a cell on either side of the passage, one cell being entered from the passage, the other from the rear. At the south-western end of the blockhouse is a third, smaller cell, leading out south-westwards, where the end of the building was broken away at the cliff edge. There is no evidence that the passage led out through an end wall-face as restored in 1971 by the Department of the Environment; the original position of this wall-face, and the overall length of the blockhouse, cannot be known. It is unfortunate that the restored masonry was not made distinctive from the original.

The most surprising feature of Ness of Burgi is the wide undefended gap between the north-eastern end of the blockhouse and the cliff-edge on that side. When the site was excavated (Mowbray 1936) particular attention was paid to discovering traces of any barrier wall which had closed this gap; there were none. Admittedly, the promontory is not beyond reach of wave-scour during very exceptional storms, and archaeological deposits to the rear of the blockhouse are virtually non-existent; although the good state of preservation of the blockhouse itself implies that any further barrier wall must have been deliberately dismantled. Since the fort clearly is a defensive nonsense without such a wall, it would be reasonable to assume that the barrier once had been complete and that the present state of the structure is a quirk of survival—the assumption would be reasonable, that is, were Ness of Burgi a unique case. It will be shown however that this curious concept of the blockhouse as an isolated building which could be outflanked, is paralleled at other sites, and that we have to reckon with this being the original design.

Jarlshof, facing Ness of Burgi on the opposite side of the bay, is the most comprehensively excavated archaeological site in Shetland. It is a vast complex of settlements, of most periods from early prehistoric to post-mediaeval, with houses continually rebuilt and middens accumulating, sealed and separated by episodes of sand-blow. The site was first explored at the turn of the century, when Atlantic gales eroded the seaward face of the mound underlying the ruined house to which Sir Walter Scott in "The Pirate" had given the fictitious name "Jarlshof". Most prominent among the structures within the mound was a broch. The whole complex was acquired as a guardianship monument by the Office of Works in 1925, and a systematic research programme was begun. Successive directors included A. O. Curle, V. G. Childe and J. S. Richardson, the final phase, which tied all the structures together within a chronological framework, being the work of J. R. C. Hamilton between 1949 and 1952; his monograph publication appeared in 1956.

The Jarlshof broch was surrounded by an outer ring-wall and was preceded and succeeded by domestic structures. Unfortunately however, the crucial period during which broch architecture presumably was developing, was not represented in the stratigraphy. An early iron age homestead was followed by a thick layer of clean wind-blown sand, and Hamilton suggested that this represented an abandonment of the settlement lasting several centuries. The site was re-occupied by people in possession of the fully developed broch-building technology. Hamilton's suggestion was that the abandonment had been caused by political troubles associated with the arrival of new and aggressive bands of settlers. Ness of Burgi he saw as a beachhead and military base established by these settlers during their subjugation of the southern mainland of Shetland (Hamilton 1968, 74). Here, then, is a suggested historical context for the largest of the blockhouse forts, a context within the most comprehensive archaeological sequence so far obtained from a single site in Shetland.

The Jarlshof excavations did not, therefore, throw light on the major problem of the origin and development of brochs. This became the objective of another major excavation, undertaken by Hamilton in 1953-7 at the broch site in Ministry of Works guardianship at Clickhimin. Clickhimin is a complex fortification; the site, on a small promontory in a loch, is enclosed by a ring-wall within which are the broch and the second of the three well-known blockhouses (fig. 5). If this structure was contemporary with Ness of Burgi, it implied that Clickhimin had an archaeological sequence of occupation which would bridge the Jarlshof hiatus. Being a notably upstanding structure close to the main town of Shetland, Clickhimin attracted the attention of the early antiquaries and it was one of the first sites to be given protection under the Ancient Monuments Act of 1882. A difficulty arising from this early interest is to know how much of the present appearance of the structures, is due to restorations which are inadequately documented and, like the recent one at Ness of Burgi, in drystone very difficult to detect.

The Clickhimin broch rises for much of its circumference from a great apron of masonry, and is notably irregular in plan. It stands in the middle of an elliptical ringwork, the entrance to which is on the south side, while the broch itself has a west-facing entrance. West of the broch, between it and the ring-wall, are remains of subsidiary buildings, and to the south stands the blockhouse. The blockhouse therefore is free-standing between the broch and the enclosure wall, with its own entrance passage aligned with the gateway of the ringwork.

This is the most neatly and regularly shaped of the blockhouses, and the only one surviving more than one storey high (pl. 2). It is curved in plan, 13.1 m long and 4.1 m wide; the wall-faces have a very pronounced batter. The central gateway has the normal two-section plan, the outer section being 1.3 m wide and the inner 1.5 m; between the sections was a door designed as usual to open inwards, and to be secured by a bar running in holes in the side walls. To either side of the passage the blockhouse contained a cell, but there was no access to these at ground level. The building is preserved to a height of 3.3 m, and on its rear wall-face, 2.4 m above the ground, is a scarcement ledge formed by projecting slabs. It has the further unusual feature, almost certainly secondary, of an internal staircase rising from the western end.

The conventional interpretation for long was to regard the broch as primary, with the ringwall and blockhouse as later additions. Doubts about this sequence were being expressed in the years preceding the excavations, and were carefully set out in an important paper delivered by W. Douglas Simpson to the 1950 Lerwick Viking Congress (Simpson 1954). He suggested

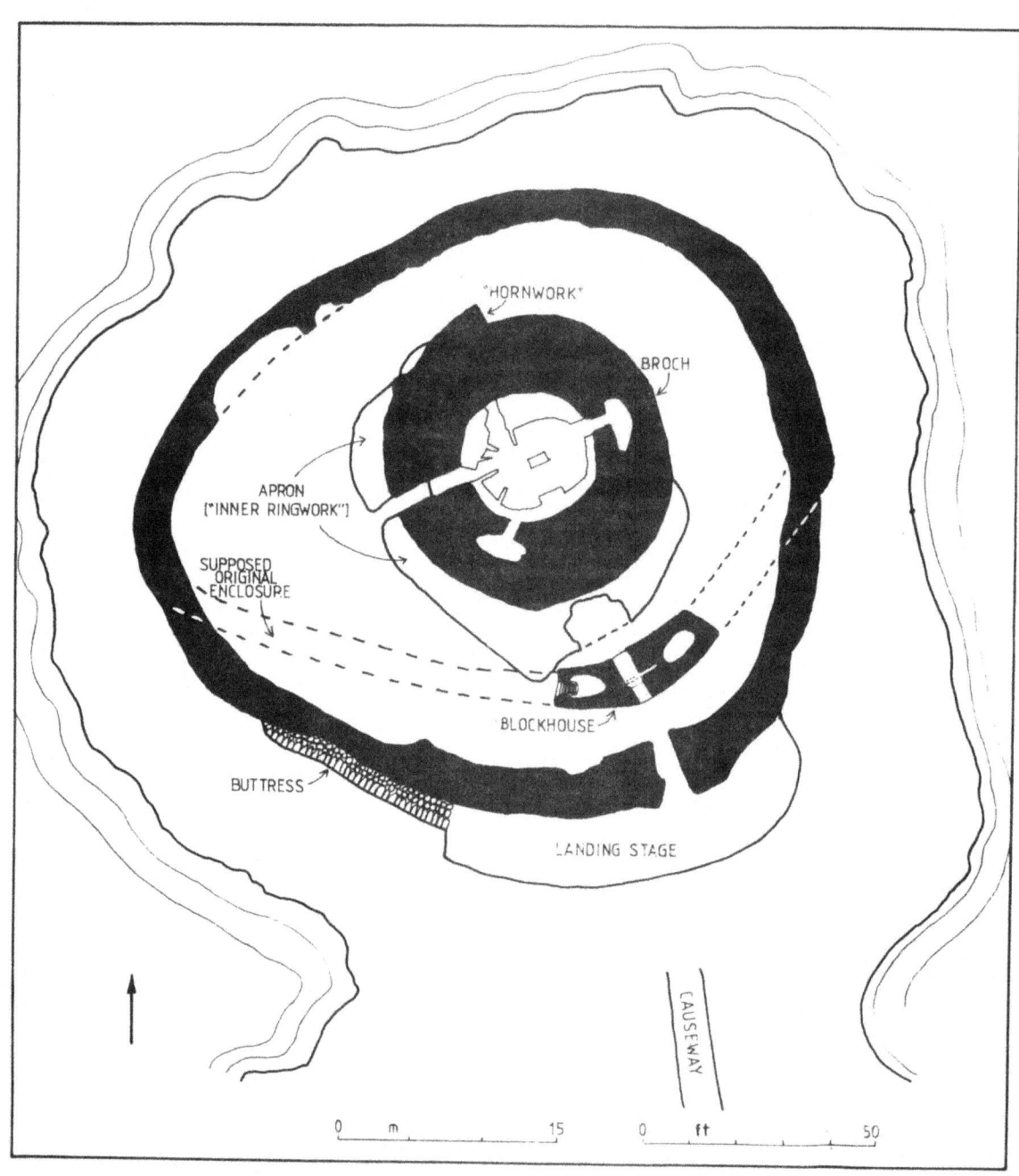

Fig. 5 Clickhimin, plan showing essential elements, with line of original enclosure as suggested by Simpson (1954). For clarity, the subsidiary buildings, which fill most of the space between broch and enclosure wall, are omitted

that the blockhouse once had formed the gatehouse to an early ring-fort which subsequently was enlarged, when the blockhouse was retained but the connecting walls on either side removed. The kinks in the ring-wall, at precisely the points where the wall would be expected to curve around to join the blockhouse, leave no doubt that some such interpretation is the true one. Simpson demonstrated that this would give Clickhimin a phase closely comparable with the surviving layout at Loch of Huxter.

Huxter, the third of the conventionally recognized blockhouses, is in a freshwater loch in the island of Whalsay; the site is a small islet close to the shore, with which it is connected by a causeway (fig. 4, pl. 3). The building remained excellently preserved until the late nineteenth century, when the stones were taken to build a school; the blockhouse had been at least as high as the Clickhimin one. It was recorded by A. Mitchell in 1881; today, the structure is in a poor state, badly obscured by tumbled stones, and evidently having suffered further robbing since Calder made his plan for the Royal Commission volume. The blockhouse faces the causeway; it is 12.5 m long and 3.35 m wide, with central entrance passage 0.75 m wide in the outer section and 1.1 m in the inner section, with the usual doorchecks and barhole. The cells on either side of the passage are entered at ground level from the rear. Although the blockhouse is built into the enclosure wall—the ring-wall running from diagonally opposite corners—straight joints show that the blockhouse and ringwork were conceived and built as separate elements, even if contemporaneously.

Archaeological conditions at Clickhimin proved to be much worse than at Jarlshof with its deep deposits and sandblow horizons; Clickhimin had been disturbed by early efforts at clearing, excavation and restoration, and on the rocky islet deposits in any case were thin. Excavation conditions therefore were unfavourable to providing clinching evidence of the relationships of the various structures, still less an absolute dating. The published excavation report (Hamilton 1968) is a stimulating and important contribution to broch studies, but controversial on many points. Hamilton suggests that the sequence at Clickhimin begins, as at Jarlshof, with a native tradition ultimately of Neolithic origin: the houses of peaceful Late Bronze Age farmers. There then was a probably peaceful immigration of Iron Age farmers who brought a pottery style related to All Cannings Cross. These new people lived in roundhouses, larger than the native Late Bronze Age ones, which at Jarlshof they overlie; the large house on Calf of Eday, Orkney, excavated by Calder and published by him in 1939, is identified with this same tradition. At Clickhimin, very little of this occupation survived. The roundhouse lay beneath the broch, and all that could be recovered was a segment of clay floor below the north-east quadrant of the broch court, and a portion of wall which was built into the much later broch wall, but partly projected outside it. This surviving masonry fragment was visible as an arc, 2.1 m long and up to 1.2 m high; its projection beyond the broch circumference indicates a wall thickness of at least 1.2 m, which information combined with the visible arc of the wall fragment, and "a thin layer of rubble round the limit of the floor deposit" inside the broch, suggested a circular hut space 7.6 m in diameter (Hamilton 1968, 34-9).

With the next period we are into the Jarlshof hiatus; Hamilton envisages the arrival of aggressive bands of Celtic, probably Gallo-Brittonic-speaking invaders, who built strongholds—promontory forts and ringworks—from which they established political supremacy over the islands. They were responsible, between the fifth and first centuries B.C., for the Ness of Burgi fort and the ringwall and blockhouse at Clickhimin, which in his chronological table Hamilton has beginning between 400 and 300 B.C. He accepts the connection with "the intensive colonisation of south-western Britain at this time by Celtic tribesmen from Gaul who introduced ring forts of the Chun Castle type into Cornwall", and suggests that the Shetland fortifications conform to a tradition of dry-stone fort-building which was being introduced into the western provinces at this period; the distinctive pottery at Clickhimin has a fluted rim with Gaulish antecedents. The original fortification was intended to be a circular ringwork incorporating the blockhouse as its gateway; the two elements were begun separately, and for some reason the plans were modified during the construction and the ringwork extended to take in a bigger area. This resulted in the kinks where the wall deviated from its planned line, and of course in leaving the blockhouse isolated within the enclosure. According to Hamilton's thesis therefore, Clickhimin had an original design very like Loch of Huxter, but this design was never perfectly carried out.

Hamilton's suggestions as to the role of the fortifications within the Iron Age society he envisages, and his reconstructions of the associated buildings in accordance with his own ideas about Iron Age social organisation, are important for the study of all pre-broch defensive structures. The suggested society is a Celtic warrior aristocracy controlling a subject population; that aristocracy would have cherished heroic ideals such as are lauded in the mediaeval Irish epics about Cet, Cu Chulainn and the rest. In a lecture delivered at Cambridge in 1964, Professor K. H. Jackson proposed that some of the material details in these epics, particularly relating to the "duns" or strongholds of the heroes, were genuine memories of the pre-literate Iron Age rather than later accretions. There is an obvious temptation to form a parallel with the Homeric epics and their established relevance to the Aegean world of the Late Bronze Age. Hamilton suggested that half-timbered two-storeyed ranges built against the inside of the fort wall, are one of these authentic details in the epics, and that these were present at Clickhimin. The literature suggests that the gate of the fort had a special significance and that the chieftain had his own quarters beside it—a circumstance which explains the elaboration of the blockhouse. Excavation inside the western part of the enclosure revealed pillar-stones and postholes traversing an arc concentric with the ringwall, associated with a hard earth floor and some paving; these buildings, it is suggested, would have provided accommodation for the chieftain's retainers, as well as byres and other agricultural functions. The chieftain himself had the blockhouse, a grand status-symbol of a gateway, built on to the rear of which was his personal accommodation. Archaeological evidence for this was a cobbled floor behind the blockhouse, and the scarcement ledge on its rear wall-face. The scarcement would have helped to support the upper-floor joists of a two-storeyed lean-to timber building. Irish laws define the entitlement of a chieftain of a given status, to a house of a certain length. Possibly therefore, the social standing of a chieftain might dictate the maximum length of the house he was allowed to build, and if a major function of the blockhouse was to provide a showpiece facade for the house, this would limit the length of the blockhouse. Ness of Burgi, which is exceptionally long (but still does not barricade the whole width of the isthmus on which it is built) may have accommodated a more important chief with a larger retinue, or the households of two related commanders.

This social rather than tactical function of the blockhouse, would explain why the Clickhimin one was retained when the original fort design was modified. In practical terms, other than looking impressive, this massive structure standing immediately inwards of the new gateway must have been rather a nuisance. So, at this stage in Clickhimin's evolution we have to imagine an oval ring-fort with a gateway facing the isthmus, within which the retainers of a Celtic warrior-aristocrat occupied lean-to buildings against the perimeter wall. The chieftain himself lived in a similar house built behind the free-standing block-house, originally conceived as a functioning gatehouse built grand to impress visitors, but which had ended up as pure status-symbol. Hamilton draws attention to a large flat stone with a pecked impression of two full-scale human feet, which is built into the later causeway. This, he suggests on the analogy of Irish clan practices in later times, was a coronation stone; possibly Clickhimin was the seat of a Celtic dynasty or at least of a noble family which had the duty of inaugurating the king or chieftain of the central island power. In the latter case, the nobleman holding the honour would according to the Irish laws be entitled to a house of twenty-seven feet (8.23 m); "though this may be coincidence, such is the length of the dwelling attached to the stone blockhouse at Clickhimin" (Hamilton 1968, 75).

Towards the first century B.C., a major change overtook the site. Possibly a south-easterly gale blowing up the Bay of Sound created a spit across the mouth of the sea loch, damming the waters and causing a rise in their level. The low promontory became an islet and its area was severely reduced; floodwater had entered the ringwork through the entrance, the threshold level of which therefore was raised. A landing-stage was created outside the gateway, and repairs and buttressing had to be carried out on lengths of ringwall where the foundations had been weakened. The peripheral ranges of buildings had been made uninhabitable and were demolished, but the blockhouse and its associated building, together with the ancient round-house which still survived on the crown of the islet, remained in use. The decision then was taken to build a new ringwork of much reduced area around the crest of the island. Work was begun on the west side of this, where a passage entrance was provided. On the north side, part of the wall of the still standing roundhouse was incorporated in the new ringwork, evidently with the intention that the roundhouse would be demolished when the ringwork neared completion. But the project was abandoned in the early stages and the decision taken to build instead a broch. This, it is suggested, resulted from the arrival of newcomers already versed in broch-building, who were closely related to the earlier fort-builders. In building the broch, as much use as possible was made of the masonry of the incomplete inner ringwork, including the part which had incorporated the early roundhouse—which still had not been demolished, and would have provided accommodation during the early stages of broch-building. When work progressed further it had to go, but left part of its wall projecting as the "hornwork" from the outer circumference of the tower. Hamilton suggests that serious defensive considerations were now paramount. The original ringwork was refurbished and the blockhouse reconditioned, the staircase being inserted into its western end. The idea was to provide a fighting platform controlling the outer gate and landing stage (Hamilton 1968, 78, 97-8).

Hamilton's proposal in summary therefore, is that the originally undefended farmstead at Clickhimin, after c. 400 B.C. became a fortified stronghold. For the first three centuries or so, this although having the design and layout of a fortress, and being capable of serious defence, was really built out of considerations of status, associated with the social aspirations of some Celtic warrior-aristocrat. In this function the blockhouse played a major role. Late in the first century B.C. a broch was built and the older defences refurbished, the site being made ready for serious defence as the overwhelmingly important considerations.

Doubts about the Clickhimin structural sequence have been expressed most cogently in a review article by R. B. K. Stevenson (1970). The stratigraphic relationships among the structures are nowhere satisfactory,.and Stevenson most notably modifies the sequence by re-interpreting the apron around the broch and the projecting "hornwork" on its north side, which Hamilton has as his inner ringwork and relic of an early roundhouse. Stevenson relates both features to a collapse and rebuilding of the broch itself. He points out how irregular is the plan of the Clickhimin broch, particularly on its north-eastern face, and proposes that it had been rebuilt inwards of its original arc, the "hornwork" being a surviving fragment of the original wallface. The "inner ringwork" apron he proposes is a massive buttress added to support the broch when it had largely to be rebuilt after early collapse. (That the tall northern brochs were not invariably structurally successful. is attested at Midhowe, where the originally ground-galleried broch subsided badly, and had to have its basal gallery packed solid on rebuilding). The "early roundhouse" therefore is removed from the sequence, and so is the "inner ringwork", a structural phase which in Hamilton's interpretation intervenes between the primary fort and blockhouse, and the broch. Stevenson's interpretation removes this obstacle against drawing blockhouse and broch chronologically closer together.

The priority of several centuries of the blockhouse over the broch, is a major difficulty of Hamilton's sequence. In its technical details—particularly the design of the doorway and the scarcement ledge—the blockhouse so foreshadows broch architecture that it is hard to imagine that these details developed very early, and then remained current for some four hundred years before brochs proper were built. Such conservatism, suggests Stevenson, is denied by "the ingenuity and vigour shown by the invention and proliferation of broch towers". A similar comment applies to the fluted-rim pottery which is supposed to characterise the early fort- and blockhouse-building immigrants; the stratigraphy being so uncertain, all of this may belong to post-broch periods.

A query is raised also about the relationship between the blockhouse and the ring-fort; Stevenson agrees that the kinks in the latter indicate that the original plan had the ring-wall link up with the blockhouse, and points out a change in the masonry at the kink on the eastern side, which confirms the theory. It is more likely that this original plan actually was executed, and that the isolation of the blockhouse is due to a secondary clearance and expansion of the fort. This is the likely context for the inserted stair in the west end of the blockhouse. The neat finish here, where the new masonry blends with the old, suggests that the eastern end also could have been rebuilt: "drystone lends itself to patching and refacing". In fact if, as Stevenson is implying, there actually existed at Clickhimin a phase when the site resembled Loch of Huxter, that parallel demonstrates that the ringwall adjoining the eastern end of the blockhouse could have been demolished without necessitating any refacing; for at Huxter the blockhouse is not bonded into the ring-wall. We shall observe this same quirk in the blockhouse fort of Burgi Geos.

The stratigraphic relationships at Clickhimin being so uncertain, and with no absolute dating, many questions arising from this excavation and its interpretation, remain open. In the absence of clinching archaeological evidence, Stevenson's suggestions commend themselves by offering a much simpler sequence than the excavator's—that there was a fort resembling Loch of Huxter; that this was subsequently enlarged so as to leave the blockhouse isolated within it; that a broch was built inside the fort; and that the broch had structural problems which led to rebuilding and buttressing. Such a development could have taken place over a relatively short period so there is no need to date the blockhouse several centuries before the broch. The two-storeyed timber ranges and the implications of a Celtic aristocratic society, likewise cannot be proved from the archaeological evidence at Clickhimin itself, but this is an interpretation of blockhouse forts which is worth consideration at other sites.

*　　*　　*　　*　　*

Ness of Burgi, Loch of Huxter and Clickhimin so far have been the only sites to which the term "Shetland Blockhouse Fort" by general consensus was applied. It is recognized however that these curious structures do vaguely resemble the massive "foreworks" associated with two promontory-sited brochs in Caithness and Orkney. Simpson (1954, 23) drew attention to the Nybster forework in his consideration of the Clickhimin blockhouse, and both Nybster and Midhowe were discussed in Hamilton's excavation report (1968, 60). The broch of Midhowe stands on a promontory formed between two narrow geos; it is the central one of a group of three brochs on a quarter-mile stretch of the coast of Rousay. The massive forework, varying between 5.8 m and 7.9 m thick, stands only 4 m in front of the broch; it runs across the promontory from Geo of Brough on the north-west, to Stenchna Geo on the south-east. Above Geo of Brough erosion has left a ragged end to the forework, so it is not possible to know whether the forework ended with a neat wall-face short of the original cliff-edge, as at Ness of Burgi, or continued right to the edge as a true barrier. At the end above Stenchna Geo however, the original end wall-face survives. Here, the forework is much increased in thickness, to accommodate a wide and much-altered entrance passage, which pierces the forework only 2.75 m from its end. At the inner end of the passage, a narrow stair, with steps cut in the rock, descends through the end wall-face towards Stenchna Geo. This end of the forework stands flush with the edge of a cliff, which however is not the cliff of the geo itself, but drops only three metres to a broad shelf of rock, 6 m wide, which then falls vertically to the geo. On to the surface of this shelf leads the rock-cut stair. The Midhowe forework, like the Clickhimin blockhouse but unlike Ness of Burgi and Loch of Huxter, has a pronounced batter on both sides. It is assumed by the excavators (Callander and Grant 1934) to be contemporary with the broch, but according to Hamilton, "it is obvious from a closer examination of the evidence that the tower is secondary to it". Hamilton rightly points out that the Midhowe forework with a ditch on either side, recalls the outer defence system at Ness of Burgi with its single, stone-revetted rampart between two ditches. At Midhowe, the excavation did not test the stratigraphic relationship between forework and broch, neither did it satisfactorily investigate the structure of the forework itself. We cannot be sure therefore that the great thickness does not contain cells or even a gallery; certainly, present ground indications suggest that there is an uncleared cell within the additional thickness of the structure, immediately north-west of the entrance passage.

At Nybster, one of the Caithness brochs excavated by Sir Francis Tress Barry at the turn of the century, the broch stands on a high cliff-promontory protected by a wall 3 m thick at its ends, with a sharp increase to 4.6 m in the middle, where is the entrance passage (fig. 6). This is just over 1 m wide at its outer end, with the usual arrangement of an increase of width at the door positions; exceptionally, the Nybster passage was fitted for two doors. On the inside of the forework, a staircase ascends against the rear wall-face to either side of the entrance, and there are traces of a gallery at ground level within the thickness of the structure.

Further examples of the "forework" idea are readily found. At Borwick, Yesnaby, Orkney, a broch stands on a triangular promontory which is barred immediately before the broch by a massively broad mound. This was stone-revetted on both sides, and at one point, probably in a period secondary both to this forework and to the broch, an irregular hut has been cut right through it. This must have happened when defensive considerations had ceased to apply. The Borwick forework is very dilapidated and fades away into grass-grown piles of debris at either end, so it is not clear whether it barred the promontory completely, or stopped short of the edges after the manner of a Shetland blockhouse. The position of the entrance is uncertain—possibly the secondary hut is an enlargement of it. A stone-revetted rampart structure seems also to have formed the main defence of the nearby promontory fort of Brough of Bigging (fig. 7), where however the dilapidation is such that the precise arrangements cannot be reconstructed.

Of the Caithness brochs excavated by Tress Barry, Skirza Head and Broch of Ness also have broad ditches across the promontories on which the brochs are sited, with a massively stone-revetted rampart immediately inward of the ditch. On this northern coast of Scotland there also are two

Fig. 6   Broch of Nybster, Caithness, RCAMS plan by A. O. Curle, 1911

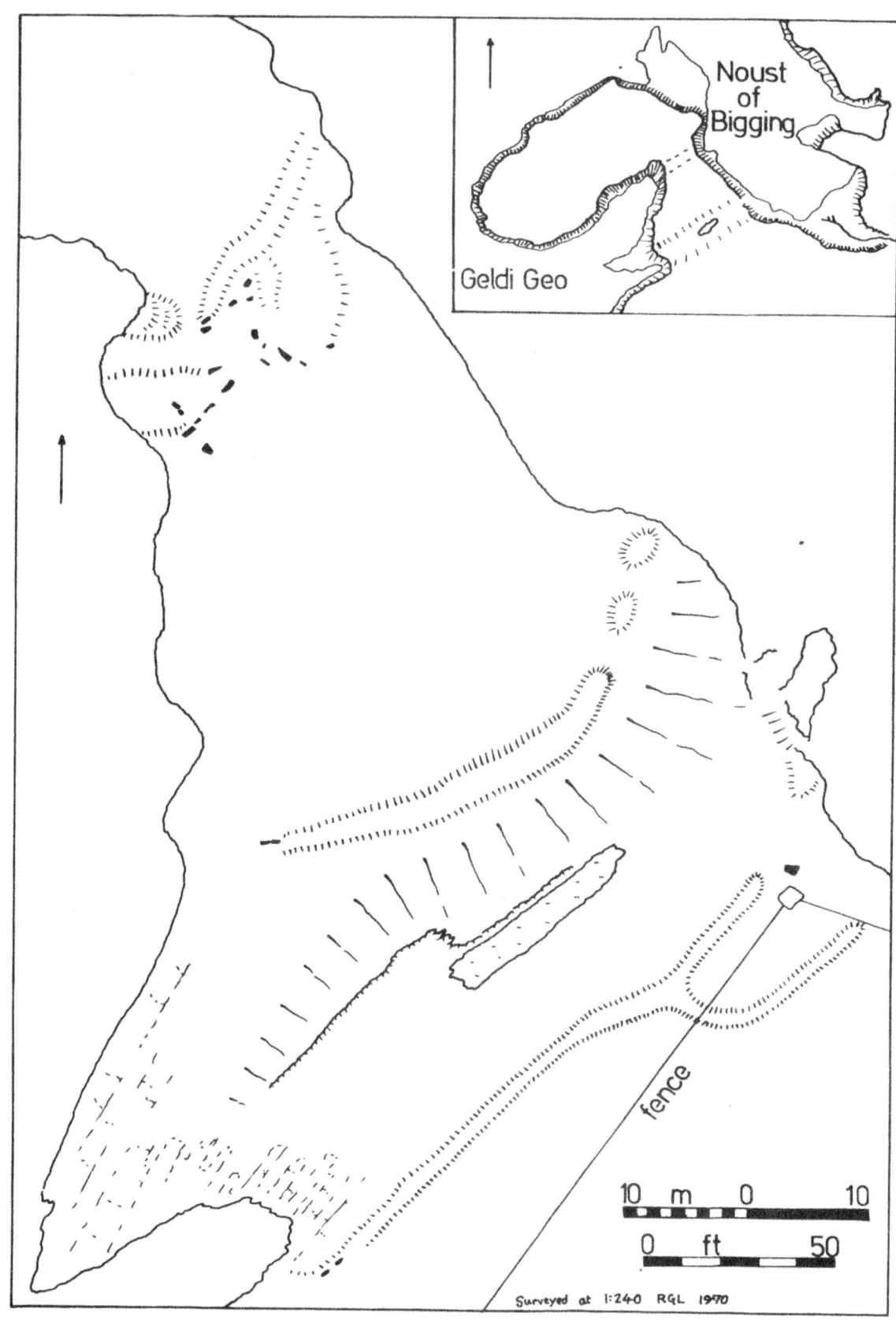

Fig. 7   Brough of Bigging, Yesnaby, Sandwick, Orkney

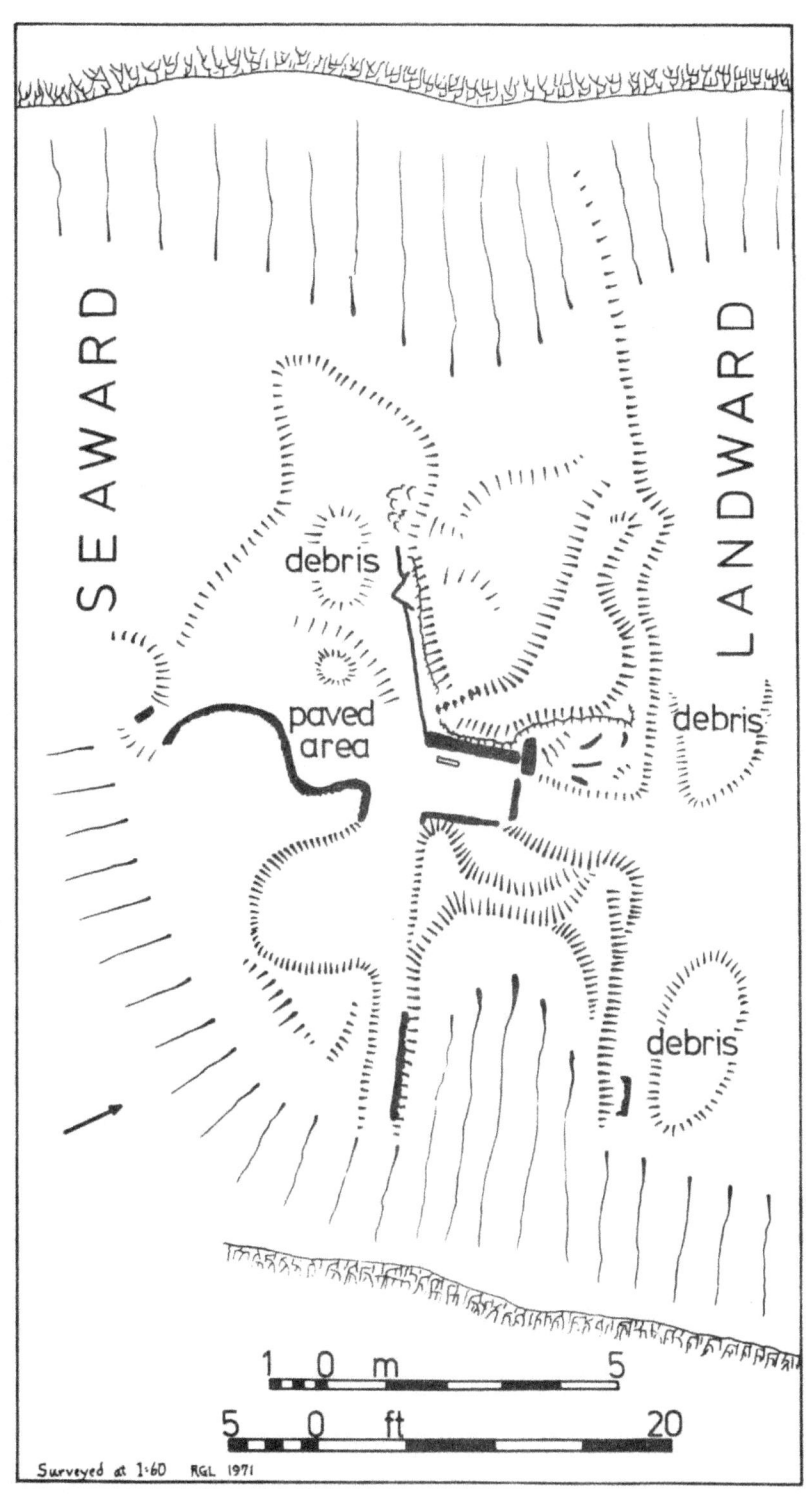

Fig. 8 Sgarbach, Caithness, plan of the wall and adjoining area

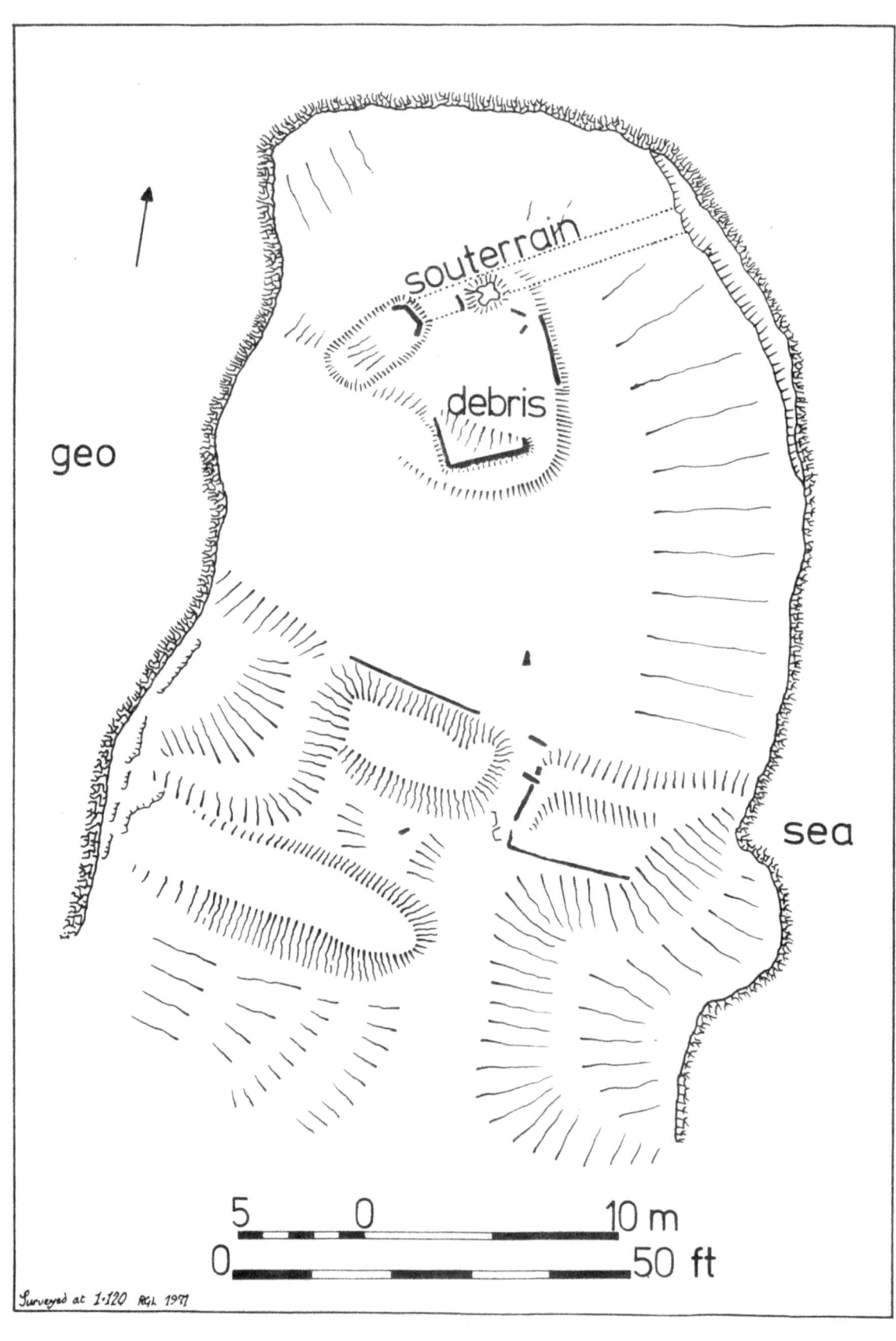

Fig. 9 Dun Mhairtein, Baligill, Farr, Sutherland

promontory forts of "forework" type, without brochs. These are Sgarbach in Caithness and Dun Mhairtein in Sutherland, important because of the strong chance that their surviving internal arrangements relate to their occupation as promontory forts and not to a broch or post-broch occupation. Nearly every northern broch is surrounded by complicated warrens of chambers and passages, often including wheelhouses, but as often as not consisting of small irregular rooms which in Orkney and Caithness are built largely of erect stone slabs. These domestic structures so swamp a broch as to destroy its defensibility, and they must relate to a post-fortification period; in most cases they will have been built of materials obtained by dismantling the upper part of the broch, for which there is evidence at Jarlshof. At Midhowe and Nybster these secondary structures are crammed between the broch and the forework, so it is unlikely that any structures behind the forework are to be associated with the forework itself. At Sgarbach and Dun Mhairtein there is much less likelihood of this, because the broch at any rate is absent.

Sgarbach was excavated but so far as is known, no plan was made at the time. The defensive work is set across the isthmus of a large, L-shaped cliff promontory; the writer's plan of the structure as it appeared in 1971 shows it obscured by mounds of overgrown excavation debris (fig. 8). Fortunately, the essential details were recorded in his usual meticulous way by A. O. Curle, who visited the site for the Royal Commission not long after the excavation. He gives the wall-rampart a thickness of twelve feet six inches (3.81 m), a length of sixty-two feet (18.9 m) and a height of five feet (1.22 m). The medially-placed entrance passage was well-preserved at the time, but having been left open for sixty years, now is almost entirely broken down. No better description therefore can be offered than that of Curle: "a passage ... 3'2" (0.97 m) in width at the outer end. At 6'8" (2.03 m) inwards on the right (the left side is broken down) is a rebate for a door faced with a slab 6" (0.15 m) thick, set edgewise in the wall, the passage in rear of it widening to 4'9" (1.47 m). Across the passage, in front of the door check, projects a sill 8" (0.2 m) in height. Behind the rebate a bar hole 8" (0.2 m) square passes for a distance of at least 3'6" (1.07 m) into the wall. At the inner end of the passage, and to the left, some 4' (1.22 m) back from it, is an oval chamber measuring some 10' by 7' (3.05 m by 2.13 m). In rear of the entrance was found a hearth defined with flags set on end, in which there were ashes, food refuse, and fragments of pottery. A drain passes from the interior outwards below the floor of the entrance passage" (RCAMS 1911, 18, no. 45). There is in fact a stone-flagged surface to this area immediately inwards from the entrance passage, so it appears that the main domestic activity on this site (there are no signs of structures elsewhere on the promontory) was immediately behind the rampart; the gateway in fact seems to have led directly into the living area.

Dun Mhairtein is a precipitous cliff promontory about 27 m high, some 200 m north-north-east from the crofting township of Baligill (fig. 9, pl. 4-5). It curves parallel with the mainland, from which it is separated by a precipitous geo. The fortification cuts off the tail of the promontory, enclosing an area some 22 m x 24 m, which is overlooked by the higher cliff on the mainland side of the geo. The main feature is a stone-revetted rampart varying between 4.9 m and 5.8 m in thickness, pierced slightly east of centre by an entrance passage 1.02 m wide at the outer end and widening inwards. An upright slab set at right angles to the east wall of the passage, forms a doorcheck. The ends of the rampart fade away towards the cliff-edge. In front of this defence the ground has been scooped back from either edge, leaving a causeway 2.5 m wide in line with the entrance. On the west side only a bank, apparently of loose material and unrevetted, intervenes between the rampart and the scooped ditch; it is about 3.6 m thick and is separated by a gap of 3 m from the rampart. The scooped ditch on this side descends to the brink in three broad steps. Within the fort is a complex of structures forming a mound, some 8.3 m back from the rampart. In this mound part of a hut interior has been exposed quite recently, presumably by an amateur excavator; the hut is rectilinear, the visible portions being the whole length of one inside wall, 2.74 m, and portions of the adjoining walls. The rest of the interior is choked with debris; the construction is good, the lower part of the wall being of orthostats, with fine dry masonry above. To the north-west of here, 3 m away, is a deep depression giving access to a souterrain which runs north-eastwards and downwards (following the ground slope) for 10.7 m, emerging on the cliff face.

It appears then that in Orkney and on the north coast of Scotland we have several fortifications which, in that they are massively broad structures with vertical or battered masonry faces front and rear, resemble the Shetland blockhouses. All of them are wide enough to contain cells or galleries but whether any actually do so, is known only at Nybster, where there is a gallery, and Mihowe, which appears to have a cell near the entrance. Whether any, like Ness of Burgi, stopped short of completely barring the promontory, also is in doubt; only at Midhowe is an end wall-face preserved. But the general impression they give, is of seriously defensible promontory forts designed as complete barriers. Because of broch-period and post-broch disturbance, original interior arrangements of the forts are not discernable except in the broch-less examples of Dun Mhairtein and Sgarbach; and at Sgarbach, the concentration of domestic activity immediately behind the rampart and inward of the gateway, is interesting in view of Hamilton's interpretation of the blockhouses.

* * * * *

The true "Shetland Blockhouse" type may be defined apart from these "forework" structures, by its end wall-faces giving it a self-sufficient appearance. At Ness of Burgi, it probably was built free-standing; at Loch of Huxter, it forms part of a continuous defensive circuit but is built separately from the contiguous walls. At Clickhimin the blockhouse began like the Huxter one, but when alterations made it redundant as a gateway, it was carefully retained as a free-standing structure. This quirk of design can be elaborated by introducing two further Shetland examples of blockhouse forts—Burgi Geos and the North Fort of Scatness—and a possible one, Riggan of Kami, on the east coast of Deerness in Orkney.

Burgi Geos must be discussed at some length, for it is a most extraordinary site; and although it has been known since the middle of last century, the practical difficulties and physical labour of reaching this remote spot on the deserted West Neaps of Yell, have preserved it from detailed publication. North and south along the cliff-coast there is no access to any safe landing by boat; and the entire hinterland of the fort is a dark peat moor. This is the notorious Yell peat, the thickest peat cover in Shetland, which on hillsides and hilltops has been eroded by water and wind into a series of gullies and mesas; the vertical sides of these are often a metre or two high, making this a most difficult country to cross. Much of the Shetland hill country is covered with the field systems and farmsteads of early prehistoric settlement; on such areas peat formation has taken place within the last three thousand years. Whether the Yell peat up to 10 m thick, conceals such an ancient farming system, is not known; but it is improbable unless the peat growth is phenomenally rapid. It is difficult to believe that the land around Burgi Geos was any better than now, at the time the fort was occupied. The nearest modern settlement to Burgi Geos has been the very marginal croft of Vigon, one kilometre to the north, which appears to have been settled and abandoned during the nineteenth century. Vigon must have depended largely on the narrow belt of grass sward along the clifftops, which although stunted by salt spray, provides better pasture than the peat moor. At Burgi Geos, the jagged cliffs of quartzite-veined muscovite-gneiss are some 60 m high; the site is the narrow sinuous promontory between the North and South Burgi Geos. The approach runs along the narrowing isthmus, where the outer defences are placed; then crosses a lower and narrower saddle of rock before climbing to the fort proper.

This is the romantic and improbable setting of one of the strangest fortified settlements that the mind of man has conceived. The outer defences, on the isthmus landward of the saddle, comprise two distinct features on each side of the path, which therefore takes the form of an avenue (fig. 10, pl. 6-7). On the north side, there is a continuous line of boulders presenting an even face to the path. On the south side, first there is a free-standing mound, trapezoidal in plan; then comes a gap, then a bank running alongside the path for the rest of the way until the descent to the saddle begins. This bank has no revetment but is set with many jagged stones which form a solitary far-northern example of chevaux-de-frise (pl. 8). The stones are set in the summit and on both slopes of the mound; on its south side, the mound slope merges into the ever-steepening ground slope which presently becomes a cliff. The continuous line of the boulders north of the path is best explained as the revetment of a bank of loose material which has slipped over the vertical cliff behind. The arrangement on the south side has no obvious logic.

Across the saddle, the path climbs steeply to the flat surface of the promontory, where it passes alongside the main structure. At first glance, this appears to be a wall of masonry running along the brink of the vertical cliff facing east, and on the south side turning at right angles to flank the path. To the north, it curves around to follow the clifftop. On closer inspection it is seen that there is a joint in the masonry about 4.25 m from the north-east angle of the cliff, and that this corresponds with a marked break

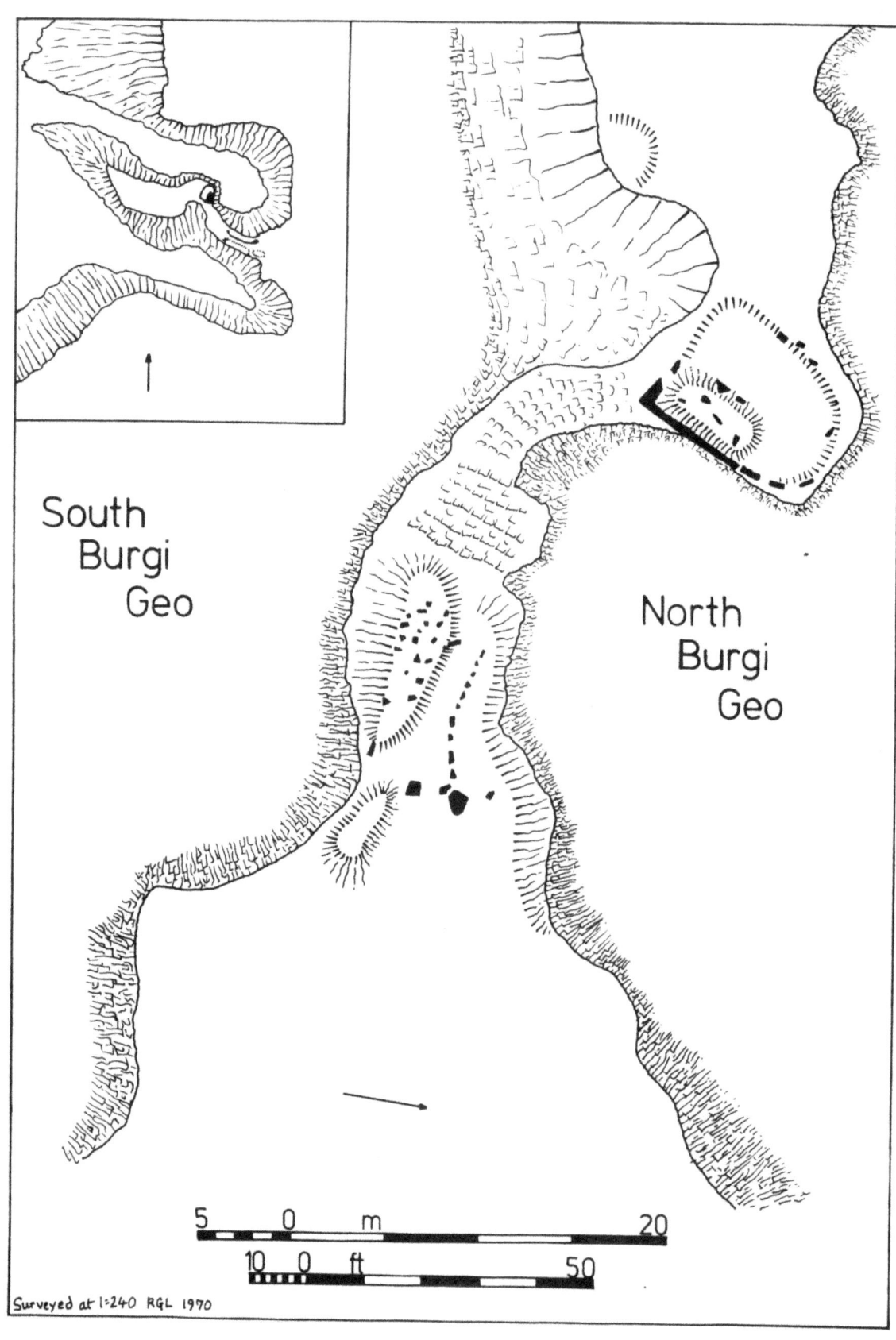

Fig. 10 Burgi Geos, West Neaps, Yell, Shetland

of slope in the mound behind it. This is shown most clearly in Irvine's sketch of 1853, fig. 11. The mound is 1.5 m high and has many projecting stones; and traces of another wall-face can be seen at its rear. The structure thus resolves itself into a block of masonry 4.25 m wide and 6.7 m long, with a wall running flush with its front face from its north-east corner, but not bonded into it; and curving around and back as a small ring-wall, to meet the south-west corner of the block, where the ring-wall is flush with the block's south wall-face (pls. 9-10-11). This is precisely the arrangement of Loch of Huxter, where the ringwall runs from diagonally opposite corners of the blockhouse, to which it is not bonded. The Burgi Geos blockhouse is wider than the Huxter one, and corresponds closely in width to Clickhimin. Bearing in mind that even the narrow Loch of Huxter blockhouse contains cells, and that the appearance of the Burgi Geos mound suggests tumbled debris, it is likely enough that here we have another example of a hollow blockhouse. But significantly, Burgi Geos does not contain an entrance passage; and it does not obstruct the path on to the promontory, the path which simply passes beside it. There is no sign of there ever having been a barrier here; no sign of masonry south of the path, no trace of the distinctive doorchecks. The site is so remote, and such would be the difficulty of removing stones, that we cannot conjure up quirkishly selective stone-robbing to explain the removal of an imagined former barrier. In any case, the parallel with the Huxter layout should leave us in no doubt that the Burgi Geos blockhouse and ring-wall are a complete unity.

The area enclosed by the Burgi Geos ring-wall is much smaller than at Loch of Huxter. From the rear of the blockhouse to the ring-wall behind it, is only 4 m. On the occasions of visits by the writer during the dry summers of 1970 and 1971, the short turf of the promontory summit was entirely parched, except in two small areas which remained lush and green. One of these was a rectangular patch immediately behind the blockhouse, occupying the space between it and the ring-wall behind, suggesting the presence of occupation deposits here. The other green area was a semicircular depression on the cliff edge further along the promontory. In the section here is 0.23 m of sterile peat overlying an occupation deposit containing some pieces of a coarse black steatite-and mica-tempered pottery (some sherds of which are now in Lerwick museum). The depression appears to be half of a circular hut. — On this promontory therefore we have a small blockhouse-and-ringwork structure comparable with one which probably existed at Clickhimin and still survives at Loch of Huxter. But whereas at Clickhimin and Huxter this layout fits the site—an approximately circular islet—at Burgi Geos it is strangely placed at one side of the approach to a promontory. Like the Ness of Burgi blockhouse, it does not barricade this approach; it does not form an obstacle against access to the promontory, where there was at least one hut in occupation.

The disposition of the outer defences is equally curious. Superficially, the function of the avenue might seem to be to confine a rush attack in a narrower space. Against a missile attack this would not be much help, since the defenders would have been as vulnerable as the attackers; but it could be some use in hand-to-hand fighting. But the construction of the elaborate avenue seems superfluous on the already narrow and dangerous isthmus,

Fig. 11 Burgi Geos: from an engraving by J. T. Irvine, 1853

where a more effective defence could have been contrived by arranging the path to run along the brink of the cliff. It seems rather that the avenue was intended to guide people along the safest path, with the stone-row to the north, and the chevaux-de-frise bank to the south, forming parapets. And it is an obvious nonsense to have chevaux-de-frise arranged beside an approach route and not across it.

The normal disposition of stone chevaux-de-frise, notably in the Irish and Iberian examples, is in front of a rampart where they would break up any attempted rush attack. It could perhaps be suggested, that Burgi Geos in its original design had a rampart—of which the northern stone-row is the revetment—to which the chevaux-de-frise formed an outer defence. This theory necessitates imagining that the original shape of the isthmus has been drastically altered by cliff-falls, so that the approach which formerly was at right angles to the two lines of defence, now runs between them. It is a difficult hypothesis to uphold. The amount of erosion it is necessary to assume, seems much too great for this very hard rock. The chevaux-de-frise bank shows no sign of ever having curved around to block the present approach. And any attempt to produce a militarily meaningful layout results in a very contrived plan. Since the inner structures of blockhouse and ring-wall make no military sense, it should be no surprise that the outer defences do not do so either. The avenue has features which suggest that it is the intended line of approach. The northern stone-row terminates at its eastern end in a particularly massive boulder, and immediately opposite this is another boulder set into the side of the trapezoidal mound. Further west along the avenue, there is an erect slab set at right angles to the path, in the side of the chevaux-de-frise mound. At both these points there may have been gates or light barriers across the avenue.

Burgi Geos has the only certain example of chevaux-de-frise for some 500 km in any direction. It is extraordinary that this exotic feature appears on so wild and remote a stretch of coast. Examples of stone chevaux-de-frise occur in southern Scotland, Ireland, Wales and Iberia; but Harbison (1971) has rejected the old idea that the British and Iberian ones are directly linked. He proposed that all are offshoots of an idea originally conceived in timber somewhere in Central Europe, possibly during the eighth or seventh century B.C. as a reponse against the increasing use of the horse in warfare. Such wooden chevaux-de-frise are represented in Britain at South Barrule on the Isle of Man. Harbison's thesis depends on the assumption that far more of these timber examples existed on the Continent, than have been found. There are no stone chevaux-de-frise on the Continent outside Iberia, and the nearest to Burgi Geos within Britain are in Midlothian and Wigtownshire.

Whether or not we accept Harbison's theory of the origin of chevaux-de-frise, it is clear enough that the inspiration for Burgi Geos was within Britain. The sheer muddled thinking implicit in the Burgi Geos layout shows that it must have been copied from a stone example—it was not the work of some enterprising pioneer who first translated sharpened stakes into jagged stones. Chevaux-de-frise have a markedly western distribution, so it must be assumed that Burgi Geos was inspired by examples in south-east Scotland or the Irish sea area. The site therefore is a clear illustration of the distances over

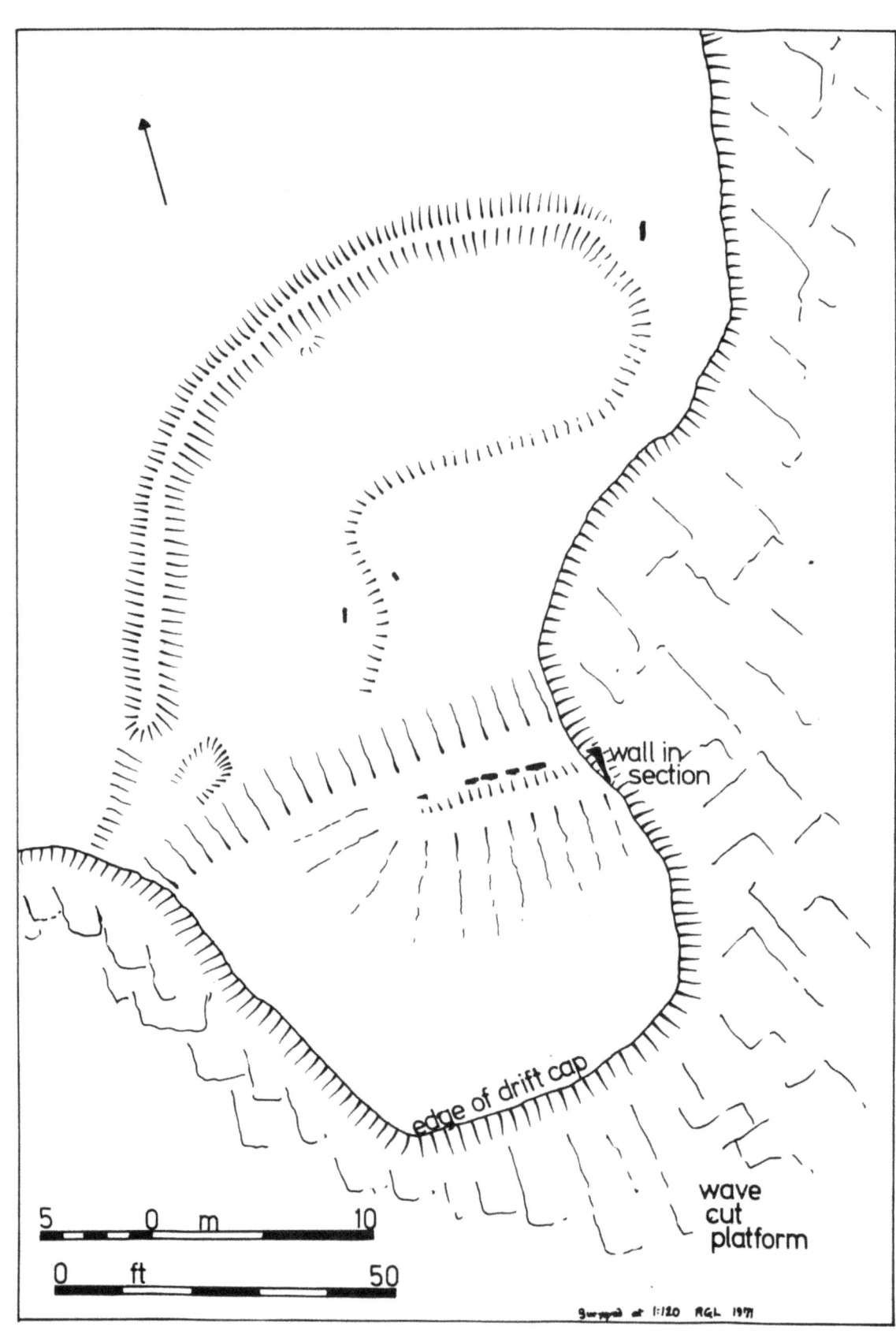

Fig. 12 Scatness North Fort, Dunrossness, Shetland

which ideas could be transmitted via the western seaways. But the builder of Burgi Geos knew only what a chevaux-de-frise defence should look like, and that it was correct to have it outside your fort; he did not understand or care about the tactical application of the thing. Having decided on chevaux-de-frise, he had to provide the earth bank to put the stones in; for with the impossibly hard rock just beneath the turf, this was the only way of holding the stones erect.

The whole impression of Burgi Geos is that is was built for prestige. Its outer approach is not a defence, but a formal avenue beside which the wildly exotic feature of chevaux-de-frise—doubtless the ultimate status-symbol of its day—is set out like a flower bed. The blockhouse is just a rectangular block of masonry not even pretending to be a gateway. The ringwork while paralleling the design of those at Huxter and Clickhimin, encloses so small an area, and is so weak in construction, as to be no more than a toy. The puzzle is, why this extraordinarily wild spot was chosen by the prestige-conscious builder. Why, if serious defence did not matter, this horrifyingly dangerous eyrie between two fearsome gulfs? Was the exhilaration of the clifftop position an essential ingredient in the desired effect?

The North Fort of Scatness lies on the east side of the Scatness peninsula, only 400 m north from Ness of Burgi (fig. 12, pl. 12-13). It occupies a blunt promontory immediately on the mainland side of the boulder-beach; anyone walking to visit Ness of Burgi must walk within sight of the fort, so it is very surprising that it went so long unrecorded. The drift cap of the low-lying promontory has been reduced by erosion even more than at Ness of Burgi, and its continuation seawards as an extensive wave-cut platform suggests that the fort interior originally was more extensive than now. An outer bank 1.5 m high and 3 m broad at base, curves inland from the edge of the low cliff in a broad arc to enclose the promontory. It is made of loose material derived from a shallow internal quarry-scoop. To the promontory itself there is a sharp rise of about a metre, and at the top of the rise is set a rectangular block. The block is grassed over but the facing stones are visible at the front. To the rear, it grades into the natural slope of the ground, so it is possible only to estimate that the width of the block was between 3 m and 6 m. At the east end the block ends on the cliff-edge, but on the west side it is quite clear that the block stops well short of the edge, leaving an undefended gap. The east end of the block visible in the cliff-section, is a wall made of large orthostats with masonry above. As there is no sign of doorchecks, this must be the end of the blockhouse and not the side wall of an entrance passage (pl. 13). Erosion here is such that it is likely that both ends of the blockhouse originally stood well back from the edge. In its setting therefore it resembles its neighbour, Ness of Burgi; and it was like Burgi Geos in lacking a gateway.

Riggan of Kami is a promontory on the east coast of Deerness in Orkney. The promontory narrows very rapidly to a mere knife-edge. Curving across the landward end is a massive structure which is another possible blockhouse. This is one of the rich farming areas of Orkney and the land behind the fort is enclosed pasture which supports beef cattle. The promontory is fenced off, and consequently is badly obscured under nettles, cow-parsnip and long grass. It appears as a broad mound 1.5 m high, extending in a wide arc to close the approach to the promontory. Depressions, and lengths of wall-face which can be found by kicking through the vegetation, seem to indicate cells and possibly a medially-placed entrance passage; more certain is a wall-face delimiting the feature at its northern end, well short of the cliff-edge. Behind the mound are traces of two circular huts, bisected by erosion of the cliff. The Royal Commission (RCAMS 1946, ii, 243, no. 628) believed Riggan of Kami to be a broch, but it is quite the wrong shape. The account mentions that midden material had been ploughed up in the neighbouring field, and that a ruined stair had been visible in the mound. We may recall the stairs in the Clickhimin blockhouse and to rear of the Midhowe and Nybster foreworks. The scale and shape of the mound suggests something not unlike Ness of Burgi which, if it had debris piled about it and a covering of dense vegetation, indeed would look very much as Riggan of Kami does today. But final judgement must wait until the site can be properly cleared and examined.

There is a further possible Orkney site of this type, at the Brough of Braebister on the north coast of Hoy. It has an elongated mound some 3 m high running on a broad arc across the approach to a promontory. The Royal Commission suggested that the mound was modern—that there had been a broch at the seaward end of the promontory, and that when this was robbed for its stone, the unwanted stones had been dumped to form the mound (RCAMS 1946, ii, 109, no. 380). This is one of several examples of confusion caused to modern archaeologists by their own usage of the word "brough" or "broch"; it is unnecessary to assume that there was a broch at Braebister, and there is no trace of one on the seaward end of the promontory. Seaward of the mound, there are traces of slab-structures. The site is a promontory fort; portions of wall-face can be seen here and there in the mound, and although in its debris-covered condition certain identification is impossible, this may be another structure of blockhouse type.

*   *   *   *   *

Attention mus here be drawn to a curious element in the outer defences of one of Shetland's notable brochs. This is Burland, a broch spectacularly sited on a cliff-headland, so arranged that the doorway opens on to a narrow path directly above the brink (fig. 20). The approach to the promontory is guarded by a triple rampart arrangement which will be described in the chapter on multivallate forts. The outer rampart is stone-revetted both sides, the middle one is a simple dump bank, and the inner one is a different construction on either side of the medially-placed entrance gap. East of the gap, this inner line is another dump bank, but on the western side it is a very neatly-constructed wall, just under 3 m wide. The end of this against the entrance is broken down and grassed over, but on the western edge of the promontory the wall finishes some 2 m back from the present-day cliff-edge. It has a neatly masoned end wall-face. This arrangement surely must reflect the blockhouse idea, for this must have been some special reason for building this short length of stout wall. Another possible example of such a "blockhouse-plan wall" is at the Broch of Burraland in Dunrossness—the broch on the mainland side of Mousa Sound—where a similar wall, also with neatly masoned end-face above the cliff-edge, forms part of the defences across the narrow isthmus.

* * * * *

All but two of the blockhouse and related structures so far mentioned are sited on promontories; in the two exceptions, Clickhimin (in its original layout) and Loch of Huxter, the blockhouse was the gateway to an islet ring-fort. These are the only two cases where a blockhouse is integrated into a design which is immediately obvious as making military sense. And only at Huxter did this layout survive unmodified—later alterations at Clickhimin made the blockhouse tactically redundant but carefully preserved it with some other function in mind. At Ness of Burgi, the blockhouse stands isolated; it does not barricade the promontory; it could be outflanked. Any military strength which Ness of Burgi possessed, lay not in its blockhouse but in the two outer ditches with the massive stone-revetted rampart between them. The neighbouring North Fort of Scatness, where the blockhouse does not contain a gateway, is equally unsuited to serious defence. At Burgi Geos, it seems that someone assembled all the military paraphernalia fashionable at the time of its building, and contrived with them a position of minimal serious strength. At Burland, the blockhouse-plan wall surely would have continued right across the isthmus if it had been intended as seriously defensive. In Orkney it appears that Riggan of Kami does not completely close its isthumus approach, and there is an indication of a similar quirk at the gateway end of the Midhowe forework.

But as we move south from Shetland, the blockhouse-like structures do assume the appearance of serious promontory forts. The Midhowe forework comes very close to being one, while Nybster, Sgarbach and Dun Mhairtein all appear to have complete barriers. We may imagine therefore that the Shetland blockhouses ultimately derive from these promontory-sited massive wall-like constructions, but that in the course of the development, military considerations were displaced by thoughts of social status and display. In terms of construction, the Caithness and Orkney structures have many features of the true blockhouses—great width; the presentation of a vertical or near-vertical wall-face to rear as well as towards the field; and particularly, the design of the entrance passage. The three traditionally-identified Shetland blockhouses contain cells and it is not known that the Orkney and Caithness structures do not do so too: Midhowe forework appears to contain a cell near the entrance; Nybster has a ground gallery; Sgarbach and Dun Mhairtein both are massive enough to have done so. We can imagine therefore that all the structures are not widely separated in time, and that the Shetland blockhouses are a special development from them, a development related to the elaboration of some non-military function. The most reasonable explanation so far proposed, is Hamilton's, that this development has to do with special buildings erected immediately behind the blockhouses.

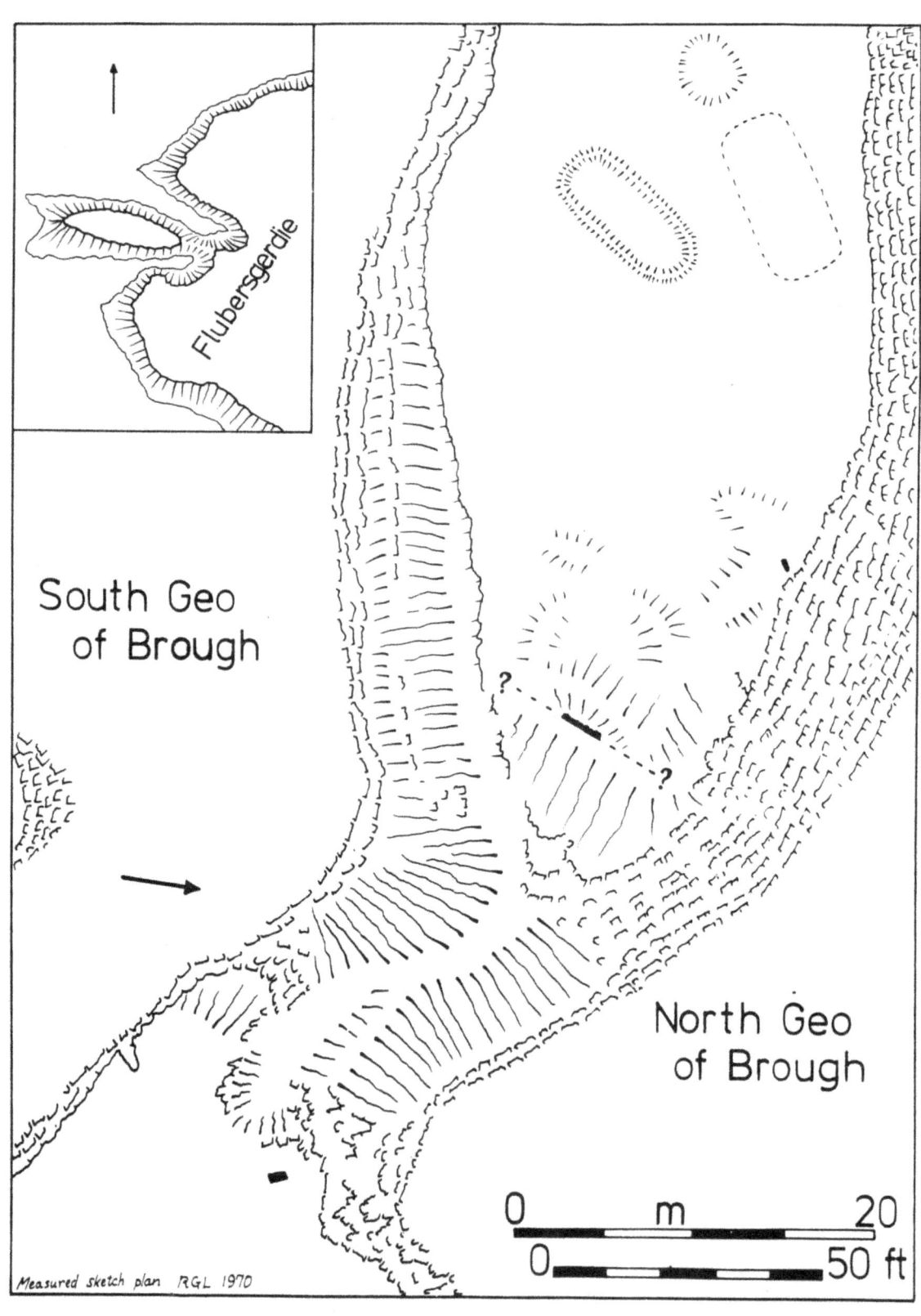

Fig. 13 Taing of Brough, Flubersgerdie, Unst, Shetland

Possibly the positioning of major buildings immediately behind the rampart, was a common practice in promontory forts. A most striking example is Dun Uragaig in Colonsay, where round huts are clustered close behind the wall (Piggott 1946). Two round huts were in this position at Riggan of Kami. At Sgarbach, the entrance passage opens directly on to a main occupation area, the main accommodations of the fort appearing to be concentrated here. At Taing of Brough, Flubersgerdie, Unst, Shetland (fig. 13), a promontory fort of indeterminate type, but possibly blockhouse-related, has its main occupation immediately behind the defensive wall. We have at the moment however no evidence of the process by which these buildings assumed such a role, that they influenced the design of blockhouses. At present, the only certain fact is that there was a lean-to building of some sort against the rear of the Clickhimin blockhouse—this much is clear from the scarcement ledge. The further details of Hamilton's interpretation are disputable. The only ground evidence for the building was a cobbled surface, the limits of which were not defined. The reconstruction of an elaborate two-storeyed timber building as shown in Sorrell's drawing (Hamilton 1968, pl. IX), depends not on archaeological evidence from the site itself, but on the application to it of the Irish epic material. It is unlikely that such a building could have withstood the Shetland winds. The scarcement could have supported roof timbers rather than an upper floor, and the whole design have been much less elaborate. The evidence for a building behind Burgi Geos is if anything clearer; the survival of deposits here is likely to be much better than at Clickhimin, and it is at Burgi Geos that excavation most likely would reveal whether these rectangular buildings were a reality.

It is equally difficult to determine precisely when the blockhouses acquired their distinctive cells. These appear to have no serious function other than to save weight and materials. In this they foreshadow the basic essential of broch architecture, the hollow-wall technique; for the double wall of a broch is much more stable than would be a single wall of the same overall thickness. That the blockhouse cells have no purpose other than this engineering one, is further suggested by the varying arrangements for access to them. At Loch of Huxter, both cells have doorways opening to the rear wall-face; at Ness of Burgi one opened on to the entrance passage and the other to the rear face; at Clickhimin the cells were accessible, if at all, only from above. The cell opening to the passage at Ness of Burgi has been called a guard-chamber, and the same function has been ascribed to cells in similar positions in the doorways of brochs. These "guard-chambers" are one of the traits of the "broch culture" supposed to betray influence from south-western England (MacKie 1969b, 59). The controversial question of immigrations from Wessex will be discussed at length in a later section; but on "guard-chambers", we surely should not attempt to relate these tiny cells to the guard-rooms of English hillforts, for there really is no comparison. Within the small social unit of a broch, it surely would have been unnecessary to have a man always at the gate watching comings and goings. And the English examples of guard-rooms within hillfort gateways, are generally much too early to have influenced brochs. The cramped, dark cell opening into the passage would have been a poor vantage-point from which to guard the door—its occupant would be in a very poor position to take defensive action, and indeed would be in a certain death-trap if an enemy did get past the door.

MacKie (ibid.) suggests that the appearance of these "guard-chambers" in the northern brochs and the Shetland blockhouses, but not in the semibrochs of the Hebrides, indicates the precise point at which the southern influences intervened. But the difference between the separate cells of the blockhouses and the linear galleries of the semibrochs, is not fundamental; it is just a difference in the application of a common technique of construction. The "semibrochs" are a distinctive type of Hebridean galleried dun; they are either built against a straight cliff-edge, assuming a D-shaped plan; or they are promontory forts. In the latter case they resemble the northern "forework" structures such as Nybster and Midhowe. The most famous one is Dun Sron an Duin on its 200 metre headland at Berneray, Barra Head. This is a massive wall containing a basal gallery, sweeping in a wide arc across the isthmus; at one end is an entrance passage with a bar-hole (Anderson 1893; Hamilton 1968, 61). The gallery was roofed with slabs, and there was another gallery above it. Behind the wall is a deep rock-cut hollow which Hamilton believes to be the site of a building similar to that behind the blockhouses. MacKie has demonstrated that such forts, more particularly in the commoner D-shaped form, are the direct precursors of the ground-galleried Hebridean brochs.

The Western promontory-sited semibrochs therefore differ in two respects from the Shetland blockhouses; they have intra-mural passages where the blockhouses have cells, and they are effective promontory forts forming complete barriers, a point which seems to have been of no concern to the Shetland builders. Both promontory-semibrochs and blockhouses however may be seen as parallel developments from a massively thick stone-wall promontory fortification, represented in the North by Sgarbach and Dun Mhairtein but found throughout the promontory fort areas of Britain's Atlantic seaboard. The process of the development however awaits elucidation; the derivation of the inspiration for the hollow-wall technique, from "murus duplex" and stepped-rampart forts with their walls built composite-fashion with internal facings, appears plausible (Hamilton 1968, 50-1), but we lack excavated examples of each stage of that development.

The distinction between the Hebridean semibrochs and other galleried duns and Western brochs with their ground-galleries, and the Northern brochs and blockhouses with cells, is not a rigid one. None of the massive stone-wall promontory fortifications, such as Sgarbach or Midhowe, has been excavated to determine whether it really is solid. At Midhowe, the broch itself began life as a ground-galleried one, the ground gallery being packed solid on rebuilding after collapse; this illustrates MacKie's thesis that an early ground-galleried form would have given way to the solid-based design as the brochs were built higher. But the claim that, because only ground-galleried brochs are found in the West, and the solid-based form is distinctively Northern, the West of Scotland is the origin centre of broch architecture—is an oversimplification. Not only the broch of Midhowe, but also the "forework" at Nybster, were built ground-galleried. And the fact that all Northern structures of this type are called "brochs" while the Hebridean ones are "duns", is apt to mislead us into thinking that there is a watertight regional division. Mousa is the most tower-like of all brochs, and MacKie rightly puts it at the apogee of the development; but on the mainland side of Mousa Sound stands Burraland, which has an exceptionally large diameter. Like many unexcavated brochs, Burraland's base is concealed within a great cone of debris, and the structure itself—with an accessible mural gallery at second-stage level—only appears higher up. It may well be ground-galleried; at any rate, if Burraland had happened to be in the Hebrides rather than Shetland, it unhesitatingly would have been called a galleried dun. Although it is one of the most spectacular brochs in Shetland, Burraland does not figure in MacKie's chart of broch dimensions (1965, 106); had it been included, its position on the chart would have been well within the part of the development which is supposed to have taken place in the West.

In emphasizing the distinction between Northern and Western forms, MacKie (1965, 140) has suggested that some features of the Clickhimin blockhouse betray a specific period of Hebridean influence. While the separate building of the "entrance section" (blockhouse), the large cells in it, and the solid construction of the rest of the wall, are all native to Shetland, other features—the intra-mural stair, the broch-like hollow wall of the upper storey, the scarcement, the regular curved plan, and the battered wall-faces— are Hebridean. None of these can be accepted without query. No other blockhouse survives as high as Clickhimin, so we cannot know about hollow upper walls and scarcements. The stair is an insertion; but in any event, there is a stair in the blockhouse-like gateway at Wag of Forse, Caithness (Curle 1946, 13). The possible blockhouse at Riggan of Kami appears to have been built on a regular curve, while the battered wall-face appears in the Midhowe forework. —It seems, then, that there is a common pool of features on which all blockhouses draw, and it is unnecessary to derive any of them from outside the Northern area.

If promontory-sited semibrochs are a parallel development with promontory-sited blockhouses, there is a parallel situation also in the application of the idea to a complete-circuit fortification. The simple promontory fort represented by Dun Sron an Duin, is related to the D-shaped semibrochs Dun Ardtreck, Dun Ringill and Dun Grugaig, which are full circuits; and the Shetland blockhouse was used in conjunction with a ring-wall at Loch of Huxter and Clickhimin, at Burgi Geos with a mere token one. The adoption of the complete circuit in place of the isthmus barrier, is a necessary step if the brochs are to be given a derivation from such structures. The small stone ring-fort is a common feature in Highland Britain and it is possible that the blockhouse or promontory-semibroch somehow was grafted on to it. At Wag of Forse, there is a circular ring-fort incorporating an entrance block through which the passage runs, with a stair opening on to the passage. This differs from the blockhouses in that the structure does not project forwards beyond the curve of the wall, which externally it does not interrupt, and it is of one build with the wall. At Jarlshof, there seems to have been an early ring-wall which broadened out, probably to form a similar entrance section, in which there was a cell; but at this point the structure is cut by the coast, and the rest of it has been washed away.

The absolute chronology of brochs and their antecedents remains very difficult. The simple, massive stone wall as a fortification is of very great antiquity indeed; Hawkes (1971) has traced the idea back across Europe to the very walls of Troy. In the Highlands the building of massive drystone forts continued into the Middle Ages. There is no dating for the examples in the North, nor is it known when the stone-wall defence first was applied to promontory forts. But in view of their many broch-like features, the development of semibrochs and blockhouses cannot have had a very long priority over brochs themselves, and structures such as Dun Mhairtein, Sgarbach and Nybster probably are to be dated not much before the first century B.C., if not within it. The early date for Clickhimin and Ness of Burgi blockhouses in Hamilton's scheme, is not supported by archaeological evidence, but is inspired by the desire to associate Ness of Burgi with the beginning of the Jarlshof hiatus. In the West, MacKie's radiocarbon date of 115 ± 105 b.c. for the semibroch of Dun Ardtreck, accords very well with what we should expect (MacKie 1969a).

As was outlined in the introductory chapter, MacKie's scheme of broch development places the origins firmly in the West, the sequence being from ground-galleried semibrochs to ground-galleried brochs in Skye and the Hebrides, then to the solid-based form as brochs became more tower-like in the North. MacKie is surely right in suggesting that the ultimate perfection of brochs was in the Northern Isles, culminating in Mousa. But the preceding pattern of development must have been a good deal more complex than MacKie's scheme allows, and we should think rather of a period of experiment and innovation lasting a hundred years or a little more, both in the West and in the North. During this period the Hebrides and the Northern Isles would have sustained, by inevitable maritime contacts, a mutual awareness, which however would not preclude the assertion of local preferences (semibrochs or blockhouses). The chevaux-de-frise at Burgi Geos are a striking indication of the length of such contacts, and hint at a delight in innovation for its own sake. In such an atmosphere broch architecture was devised, refined and developed; the suggestion that the main development happened in one area, and later was transferred to another, is an over-simplification.

* * * * *

The historical meaning of the blockhouses, like that of the brochs themselves, remains an open question. What does appear certain is that their construction has more to do with social display and status than with serious defensive considerations; but this does not altogether reveal the frame of mind of the builders of Burgi Geos. The site chosen here was a horrifyingly dangerous one, where a careless step could mean a plunge over a sixty-metre precipice; does this mean that there was still some concern for security from attack? It is a puzzle that this fort, built to a pattern that could only be prestigious and intended to impress, should also be so remote—entirely inaccessible from the sea, and closed in by peat moor on its landward side.

When we look at the other blockhouse forts, we see however that Burgi Geos is only the most extreme case of a common tendency. No blockhouse is strategically sited. Clickhimin and Huxter are islets in lochs—at Huxter, well inland and with no obvious recommendation for the spot, at Clickhimin admittedly near a beach, but with no obvious reason for preferring this beach to any other. It is a mistake to believe that Ness of Burgi, and indeed Jarlshof, are strategic positions because they are at the southern extremity of Shetland. Doubtless the inhabitants of Jarlshof used boats from the beaches of West Voe of Sumburgh—since they lived here, they would have known the tides well enough to ensure their safety; but the long promontory of Scatness, an out-of-the-way place to get to overland, is hedged with murderous reefs and certainly is no place for regular landings. In any case, the approach into the West Voe itself is perilous; it lies across the line of the notorious Sumburgh Røst, a race which runs at seven knots during spring tides, and the whole sea area around Sumburgh Head is beset with tidal streams of great complexity and violence which often run in opposite directions at places not far apart. The "North Sea Pilot" recommends that all vessels without local knowledge keep well clear of this area, and suggests that the røst is dangerous for any vessel smaller than a trawler (Admiralty 1949, 131-3). A safer port than West Voe used to be the Pool of Virkie, until it filled with sand late in the seventeenth century; this lies 1.7 km north of Jarlshof and nearly 3 km from Ness of Burgi. —It appears then, that the particular positions of Ness of Burgi, Loch of Huxter, Burgi Geos and Clickhimin, are only of local interest and lack any wider strategic implications, unless there was some exceptional circumstance of politics such as never will be revealed by archaeology.

This does not encourage us to accept Hamilton's suggestion that Ness of Burgi and Clickhimin were strategic bases established by Celtic invaders in establishing their rule over the islands. We have seen in any case that the blockhouses most likely developed within the Northern area, during a period of exchange of ideas with the West of Scotland—they are not a ready-designed fortification brought in from outside, like the motte-and-bailey castle in Norman England. With Ness of Burgi it surely is no coincidence that there is another blockhouse fort, of simpler design, at North Fort of Scatness, and it may be that the latter fort is slightly earlier and that Ness of Burgi replaced it.

Hamilton's claim that Clickhimin demonstrates a society conscious of social status is a reasonable one; it is so far the best explanation of the quirkish design of the blockhouses. His claim that this society was distinctively Celtic is much more dubious. The archaeological evidence for the building behind the Clickhimin blockhouse, is just about adequate to suggest that a rather special building was present there, but not to demonstrate that it was of the elaborate, two-storeyed and in Shetland winds probably unsafe design which Hamilton postulates. The continuing argument over blockhouse-buildings demands fresh evidence which best would be obtained by careful excavation of Burgi Geos, where survival of deposits appears to be good. We have to admit that Hamilton's explanation of the limited length of blockhouses, precluding their forming complete isthmus-barriers—that this length was regulated by the buildings behind them, governed by traditional laws—is so far the only one, which is not to say that it is necessarily right or that the link with the Irish laws is valid except as an unrelated ethnographic parallel. But in general, the interpretation of Clickhimin in terms of this very special, aristocratic Celtic society, is based more upon the undatable details in the Irish epics, than on direct archaeological evidence from Clickhimin itself. The best that can be said of the archaeological evidence, is that it does not contradict the Irish epic material.

That these Irish epics have a direct bearing on Shetland is as dubious as that any Celtic-speaking people ever was present there. Certainly it is remarkable, if Shetland had been dominated by Celts for some hundreds of years, that there is no trace in the place-name record. Most Shetland place-names are, of course, very readily explicable as Norse. But the example of England, where strata and substrata of Celtic, Anglo-Saxon, Norse and Norman-French—all of these languages known to us today—make up the total record, should warn us that it is highly unlikely that one introduced language could have replaced existing place-names to the extent of one hundred per cent. That we have difficulty finding pre-Norse names in Shetland and Orkney means only that we do not know what to look for—the pre-Norse language, presumably, was some form of non-Indo-European Pictish. Efforts by scholars have failed to produce convincing examples of Celtic elements in Northern Isles place-names.

The one modern excavation of a blockhouse associated with other structures, therefore has left open most of the obvious questions. The matter can be taken further only by excavation of other blockhouse sites. Ness of Burgi was excavated in the 1930s, and the wave-scoured condition of the enclosed area makes it unlikely that any good occupation evidence survives there. The same is true of the equally low-lying North Fort. This however would be worth a trial trench to discover the nature of the blockhouse, as also would Riggan of Kami. The interior of the Huxter fort is full of debris, and it cannot be known whether, under this, deposits are any better than at Clickhimin. The main priority therefore should be Burgi Geos where deposits are good and the site undisturbed. The very insecure position of the blockhouse on a badly faulted precipice—the blockhouse has lost several courses of stonework since Irvine sketched it in 1853—gives a very real rescue reason for such an excavation to be done as a matter of urgency.

III

THE MULTIVALLATE FORTS AND THE WESTERN SEAWAYS

It is well known that multivallate outworks to brochs are a feature of Shetland and Orkney but not of the Hebrides. Multivallate promontory forts so far have not been recognized as a group in their own right in the Northern Isles. This is because the forts are few and widely scattered, and because the finest examples remained for long undiscovered, or published only as sketchy outline notes. Of the four examples most rewarding of study one, the Landberg, is in Fair Isle—it is briefly described in the Royal Commission Inventory, but it is not surprising that in view of the difficulty and effort of getting to Fair Isle (and the risk of not getting off it again), archaeologists did not flock there to see it for themselves. Another important multivallate fort, the Brough of Stoal in Yell, was misinterpreted as a broch outwork. The fort at Hog Island Sound, Nesting, Shetland, was first discovered by an Ordnance Survey field investigator in 1968, while the Brough of Windwick in South Ronaldsay, Orkney, in spite of the obvious clue provided by its name, was only found by the writer in 1971. Of none of these important sites is there a previously published plan.

Considering the great distance between them, the forts of Hog Island Sound and the Landberg are remarkably similar. The Landberg occupies a commanding position overlooking the twin Havens at the northern end of Fair Isle; the site is a narrow, precipitous headland the surface of which slopes gently up from the land towards the sea (fig. 14, pl. 14). Across the isthmus is a narrow rift caused by faulting, the ground to seaward of this being higher than the land side. The slope up from the bottom of the rift to the summit level of the promontory is very steep, giving a good natural basis of defence. At the top of the slope behind a narrow berm, is a broad rampart revetted at the front with large stone blocks. Landward of the rift is a series of low dump banks made of the material from shallow intermediate scoops, the banks nowhere standing more than 1.2 m above the bottoms of the scoops. The bottom of the natural rift has been deepened by a vertical-sided cutting. Thus the defensive scheme presented to an attacker consisted of a series of low banks followed by a deep ditch, then a very steep climb up to the main rampart (pl. 15-16). The entrance runs straight through the banks, but these are not continuous in their line across the path; those on the east side form a set of three, while on the west side there is a single horseshoe-shaped bank curving out from the cliff edge to flank the path. At the western end of the inner bank of the three on the east side, there are two large boulders set beside the path. The path crosses the rift on a reserved causeway (representing the bottom before the extra cutting was made), climbs straight up the slope, and passes on the same line through a stone-lined entrance gap in the main rampart. Behind the entrance there is the foundation of a substantial

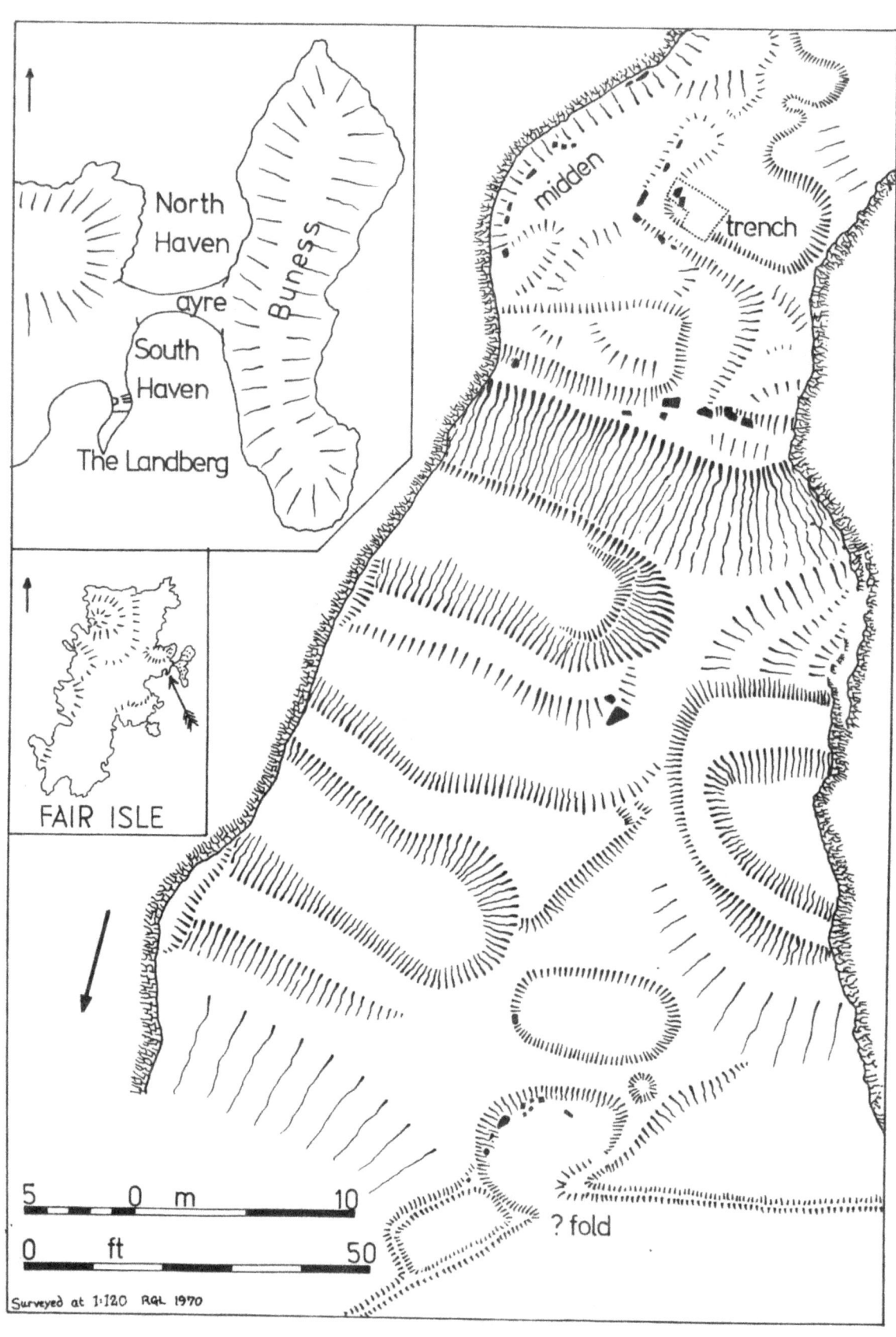

Fig. 14 The Landberg, Fair Isle

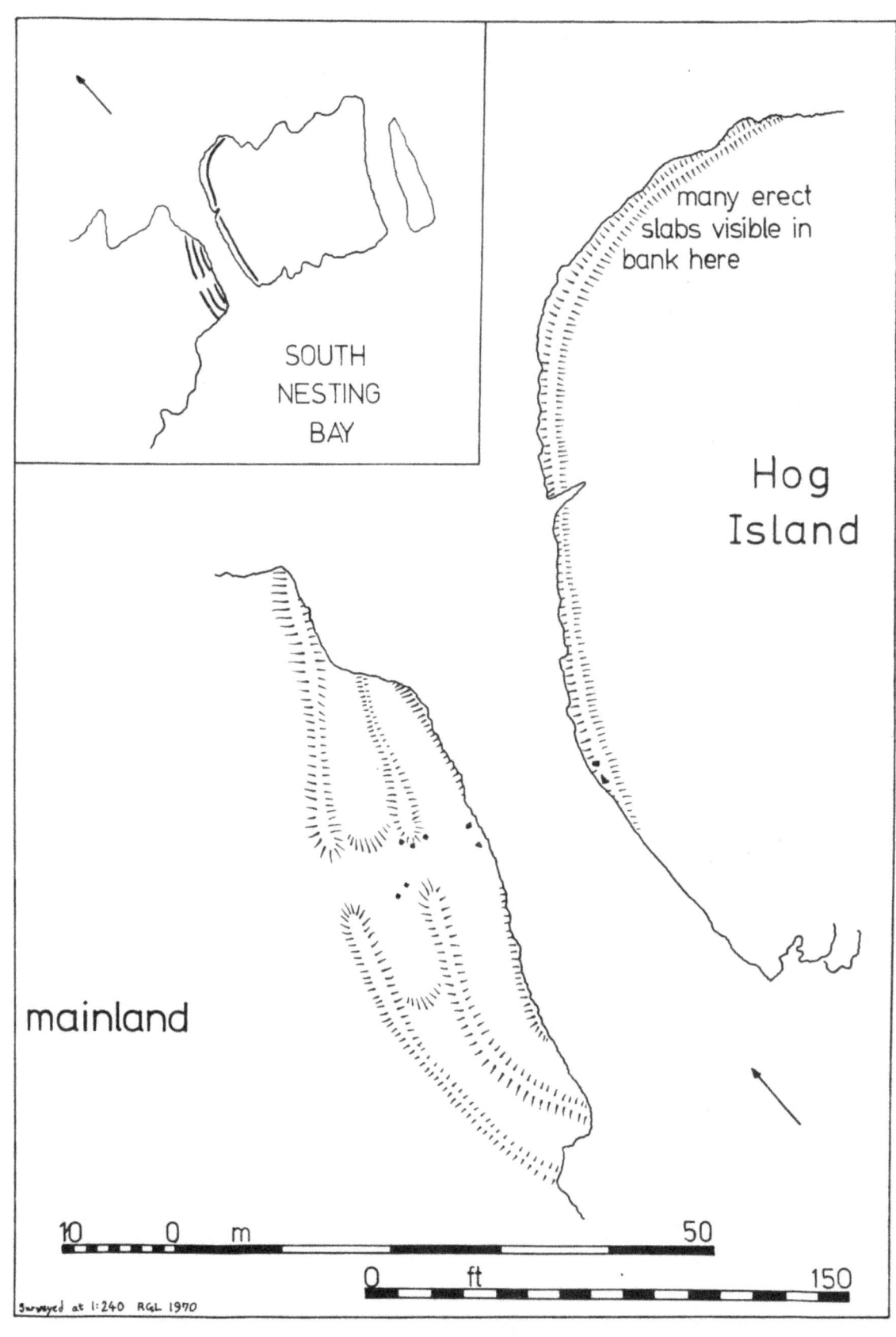

Fig. 15 Hog Island Sound, Neap, Nesting, Shetland

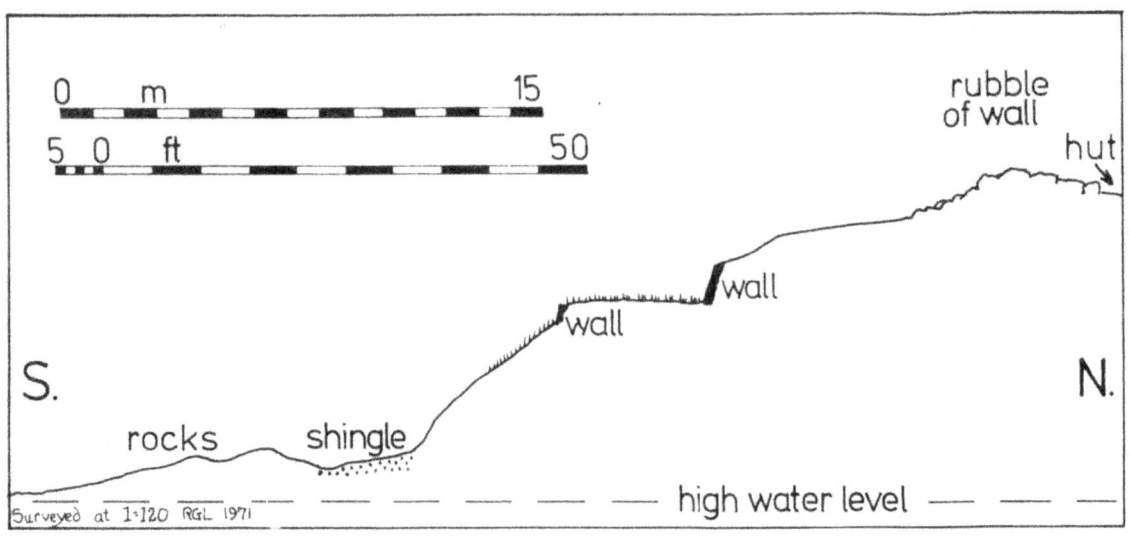
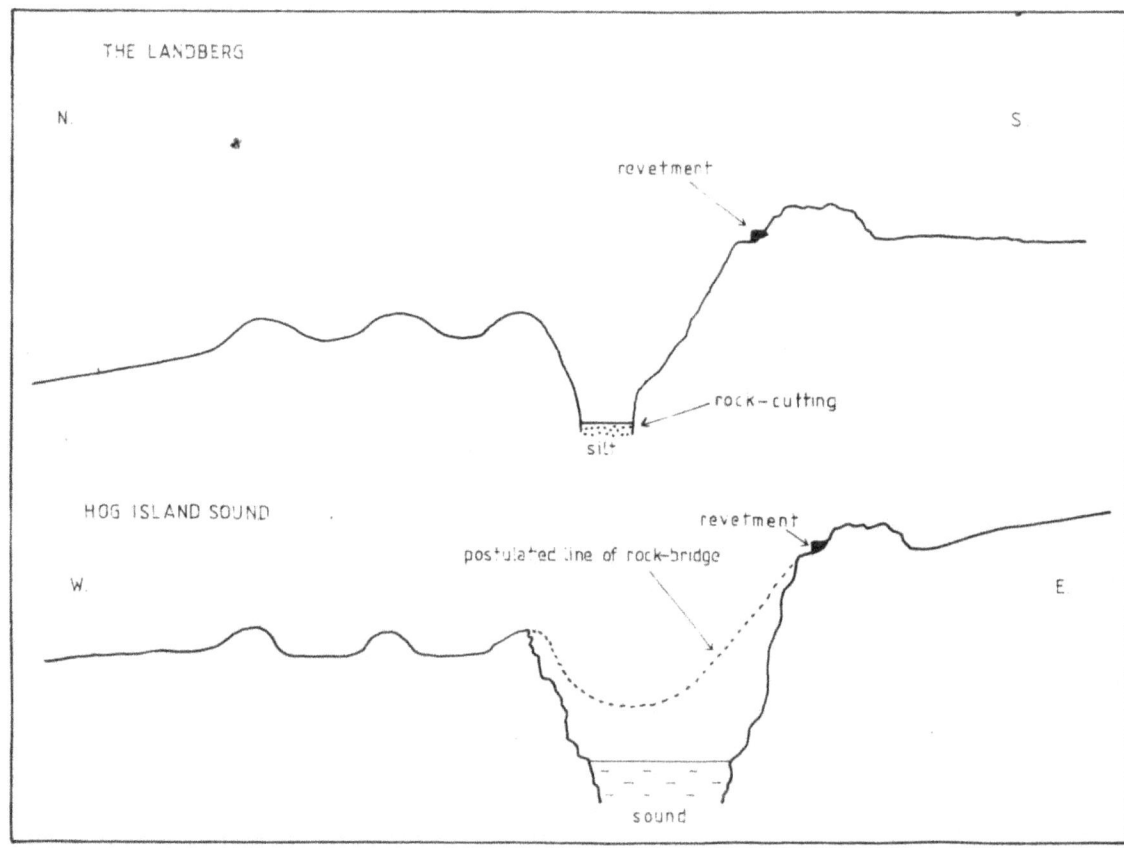

Fig. 16 (above) Profile of defences of Brough Ness of Garth, Sandness, Shetland, cf. plates 21-22 (below) sketch-profiles of defensive schemes at The Landberg and Hog Island Sound

rectangular building of stone, probably representing a secondary occupation. It is 6.7 x 4.3 m internally with walls 1.2 m thick. There is a doorway in the south side near the south-eastern corner. Someone quite recently to the time of visit, had dug an L-shaped hole into the north-eastern corner, revealing that the wall had facings of large blocks about a core of loose stones; there is no trace of mortar. The doorway leads into a string of shallow depressions which extend southwards towards the tip of the promontory. Northeast of the building the ground is very hummocky and there seems to have been a stone parapet along the cliff-edge on the east side; in this area is an extensive midden deposit.

The fort at Hog Island Sound has been cut in two by the sea (fig. 15). At the eastern extremity of Nesting the broad headland on the farmstead of Neap, is continued seawards as Hog Island, from which it is separated by a gulf 13 m wide. The cliffs are about 12 m high on the land side and 15 m on the island side. The defences now run along the brink on each side, Hog Island being the defended area; originally there must have been a rock-bridge. Along the edge of the island is a considerable rampart, in which large stones are visible; evidently it was revetted like the main rampart of the Landberg. On the mainland side are three low banks, the inner of which is cut in half longitudinally by the cliff edge. Each bank is 3m broad and between 0.5 and 1 m high, being made of loose material derived from shallow intermediate scoops (pl. 17). These are flat-bottomed and seem to represent the removal only of the few centimetres of topsoil and the uppermost, friable layer of bedrock. At the mid point the banks are pierced by an entrance gap running in a straight line through all three. There are large boulders set in the ends of the middle one beside the entrance, and the path passes between two even bigger ones in the inner bank; at this point the path now ends abruptly at the brink. Hog Island is inaccessible, boat access being possible only in exceptionally calm weather, so the portion on the island cannot be examined in detail; it appears however that the entrance passage in the main rampart was directly in line with the path on the land side.

Both forts have the same concept of a strong rampart at a high level overlooking and commanding outer defences composed in each case of three low dump banks (although modified by the horseshoe bank on one side of the Landberg) (fig. 16). In both cases only the main rampart has a stone revetment. Both situations are chosen with a break of slope giving a naturally steep climb to the summit. The entrance path runs in a straight line through all the defences and the forts share the feature of large boulders set in the ends of some of the banks, beside the path. And in both cases the material for the banks has been obtained with great difficulty, from shallow intermediate scoops.

The use of this defensive scheme raises two important points, concerning the type of warfare the builders had in mind, and the use of dump banks and ditches where the hard rock makes these very difficult to construct. The function of the outer banks clearly is not as manned ramparts—they are not big enough; and as there is very little eroded material in the intervening scoops, they are unlikely originally to have been higher. And all the banks in the series stand at the same height. Seen in relation to the main rampart

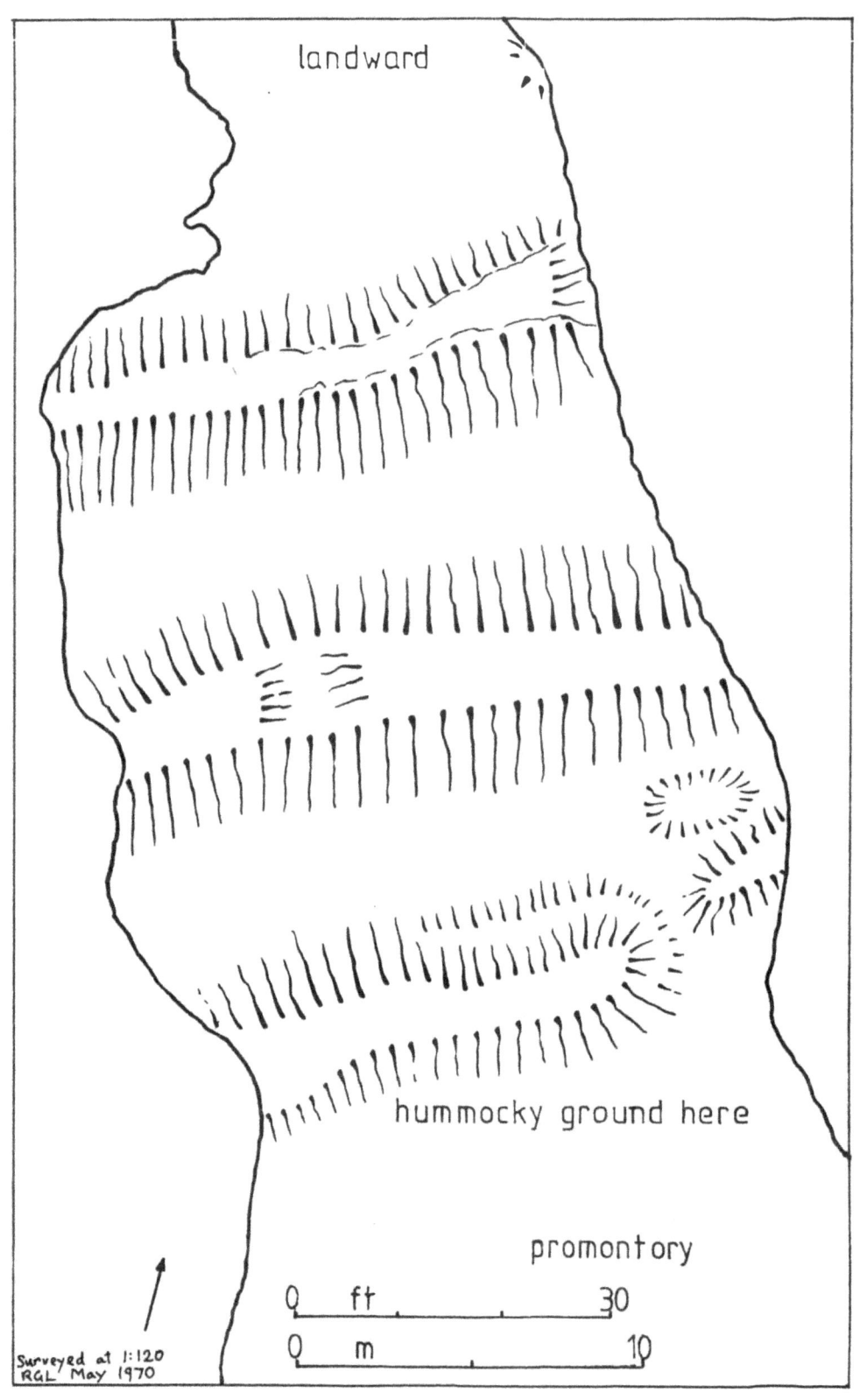

Fig. 17 Brough of Stoal, Aywick, Yell, Shetland

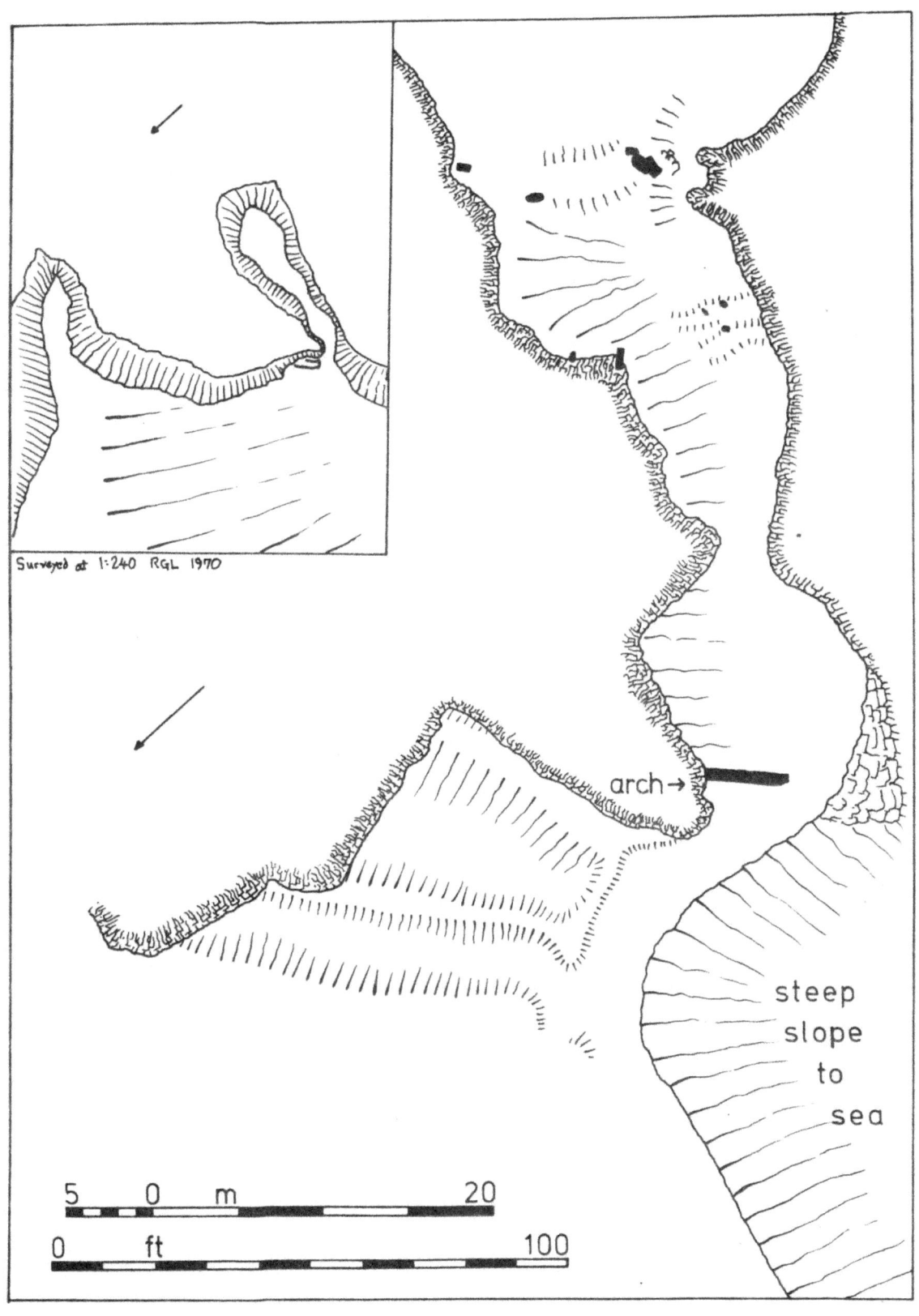

Fig. 19 Brough of Brogastoon, Lambhoga, Fetlar, Shetland

overlooking them, they assume a more serious military function—they would obstruct attackers, break up their charge, and above all expose them to the fire of the defenders above. This suggests a situation of warfare relying heavily on missiles, and inevitably raises the question of the use of the sling.

At both forts, sections through the outer banks can be seen at the cliff edge, and there is no doubt that they are dumps. There has been great difficulty in obtaining the necessary material, with a very thin soil overlying intractable bedrock. It was necessary to scour loose material from a wide area to build even a small bank, so a dump rampart more than a metre or so high, and in itself defensible, was out of the question. The "three-and-one" arrangement of banks and rampart, utilising a steep natural slope between the two elements, was a clever way of using such low and weak banks to make an effective fortification. It was an ingenious device; but it remains true, that had the builders used the stone or turf construction traditional in the Northern Isles, they could have erected larger and more effective barriers.

Where the underlying rock was a relatively soft sandstone, or there was a thick cover of glacial drift, it was possible to dig deeper ditches and make larger ramparts; in such areas we find a different type of multivallate fort. Two important ones are the Brough of Windwick in South Ronaldsay, Orkney, and the Brough of Stoal at Aywick, Yell, Shetland. Stoal occupies a high, narrow promontory sloping gradually up from the land, so that although all three of its dump ramparts are of much the same size, there is effectively an increase in height towards the interior of the fort (fig. 17, pl. 18-19). They are never less than 2.1 m high, the middle one standing more than 3.7 m above the bottom of the ditch, which is heavily silted. There was a fourth, outer rampart on the east side only, of which only a fragment survives; this may have covered the entrance which, since there is now no trace of it, must have been against the cliff-edge on one side. Within the defended area there seems to have been a complex of huts made of slabs and some masonry; but nothing to suggest the broch which the Royal Commission postulates (RCAMS 1946, iii, 161, no. 1717); it is unnecessary to assume the former existence of a broch to explain this very fine promontory fort.

The Brough of Windwick is a narrow headland projecting from the precipitous cliffs, which here as at Stoal are some 50 m high, on the north side of Wind Wick, in the Linklater district of South Ronaldsay. It has a curious defensive system involving two banks crossing the isthmus at the inner end, with a series of banks and ditches outside (fig. 18). The entrance path is central; on the south side of it the outer system comprises four scooped-out, U-sectioned ditches with three intervening banks, and on the north, two such ditches with one rampart between. This asymmetry recalls the Landberg layout, and there is no obvious military reason for it. The ramparts appear to have been built partly of turf, and retain an impressive near-vertical profile, standing up to 2.5 m above the ditch bottoms; from the bottom of the inner ditch to the top of the bank is 4.5 m. The promontory is approached on the level and the ditches appear to be wholly artificial, being cut into the thick drift cover; but the inner northern ditch at any rate, is cut through this into the rock. The area is very overgrown and no structures could be seen within the fort.

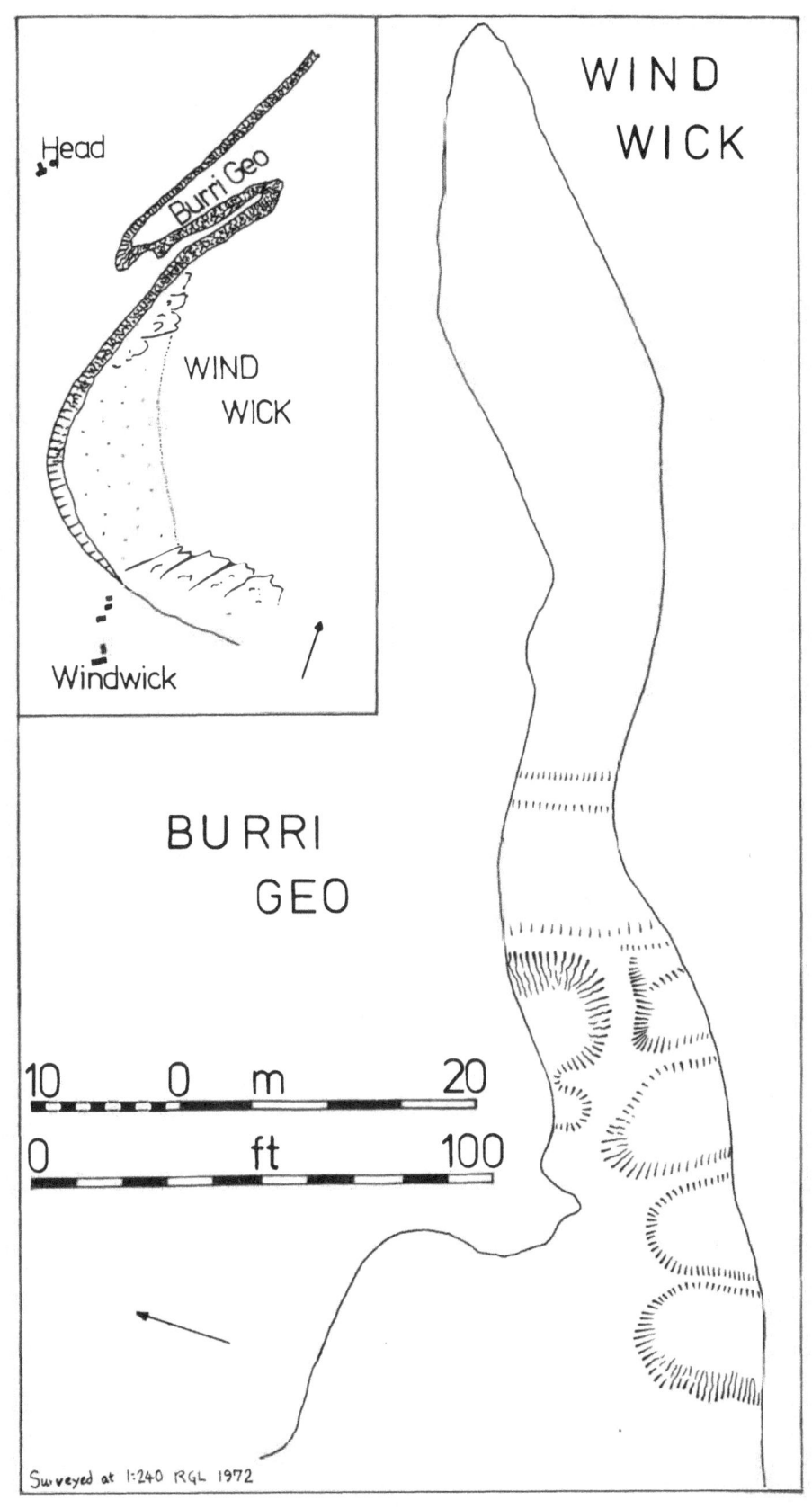

Fig. 18 Brough of Windwick, South Ronaldsay, Orkney

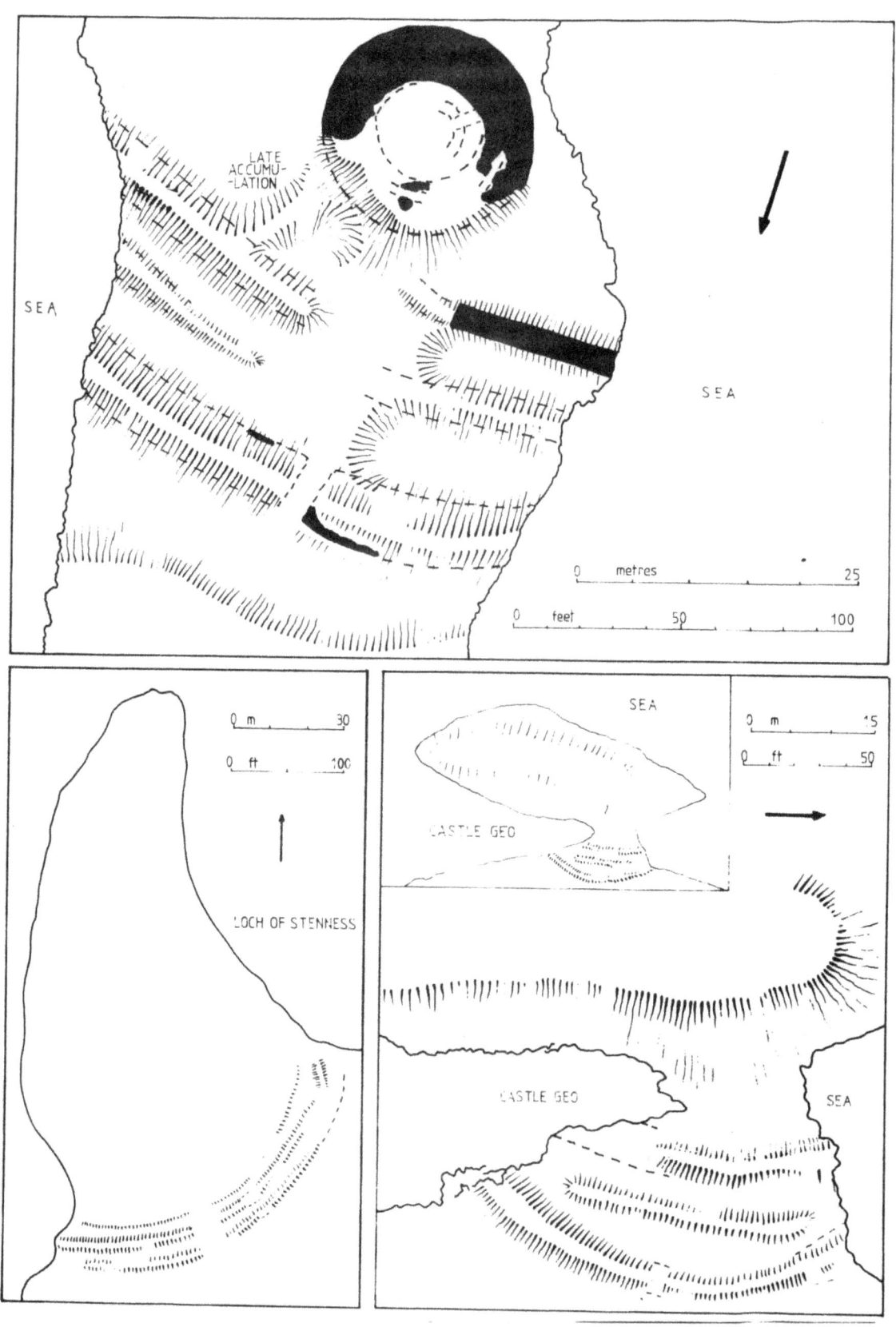

Fig. 20 (above) Broch of Burland, Lerwick, Shetland (left) Fortified promontory at Onstan, Stenness, Orkney (right) Castle of Burwick, South Ronaldsay, Orkney. RCAMS plans by C. S. T. Calder

An asymmetrical arrangement on either side of the entrance path is taken even further at the Brough of Borgastoon in Lambhoga, Fetlar, Shetland (fig. 19). Lambhoga is a long hogback covered by peat and used as a sheep-run; it contrasts with the rich and fertile condition of much of Fetlar. Borgastoon is an isolated long-abandoned farmstead occupying a few hectares of improved land at the southern extremity of Lambhoga; on the cliff-coast nearby is the narrow promontory called the Brough, the defences of which consist of two earth banks each fronted by a ditch, extending nearly across the isthmus, but joined across their western ends by a cross-bank flanking the path. There are indeterminate traces of structures on the promontory itself. The original scheme at Borgastoon may have been more complex, as a lot of it seems to have gone into the sea.

The Taing of Onstan, a flat low-lying promontory on the shore of the Loch of Stenness in Orkney, is a small bivallate fort (fig. 20). It is defended by two banks each 0.6 - 0.9 m high, of loose material derived from shallow internal ditches. There is no other feature visible on the promontory, which is about 0.6 ha in area and is good-quality pasture. A section across the defences was cut during the early 1960s by the late Dr. F. T. Wainwright; this section shows a simple dump-rampart structure with traces of possible stone revetments (Ordnance Survey Card Index, ref. HY 21 SE 22). Wainwright believed that the defences were a relic of a Norse "nesnám", but no dating evidence is recorded, and it is more likely that this is an Iron Age fort. (The meaning of "nesnám" is discussed in Appendix 2).

There is a distinction between the "three-and-one" type of fort, built where the hardness of the rock precludes the digging of deep ditches, and the type where all the ramparts are of equal magnitude and stand at the same level. The latter could be built on a flat promontory like Windwick, or on one with only a slight slope-advantage, as at Stoal; but the "three-and-one" type demanded a headland with a steep natural step in it. The choice between the two designs may have depended more on the nature of the available site, than on any difference of tradition.

Multivallate promontory forts, as opposed to multivallate broch-ourworks, are not common in Orkney and Shetland; but they are just as thinly distributed along Britain's other promontory fort coasts. The only other Northern example of a "three-and-one" fort is the Castle of Burwick, in South Ronaldsay, Orkney which has three low banks curving across a narrow isthmus. There is then a sharp rise to the summit level of the promontory, the slope being crowned by remains of an inner rampart (not shown on the Royal Commission plan, fig. 20). This fort had internal structures some of which are probably secondary to the defences, but it is badly disturbed by slip-faulting, and overgrown. At Aithbank in Fetlar—a site not previously recorded—a small promontory is defended by three dump banks of equal height, much reduced by cultivation. Another fort which was at least bivallate if not multivallate, stood at the head of the Bay of Girston in Caithness, but nearly all of this has fallen into the sea. Multivallate defences around brochs however are commoner, and these are a feature of Northern brochs which is not shared by the Hebridean ones. There seem indeed to be no convincing examples of multivallate dump-bank forts in the Western Isles; a curious circumstance, in view of their occurrence in the promontory fort areas both to north and to south.

* * * * *

There has been very little modern research on coastal promontory forts in the southern part of the Atlantic area. Those of Galloway are known from the Royal Commission surveys dating from before the first world war; the Irish ones, from the exhaustive fieldwork of Thomas Westropp at the turn of the century. A partial list of Cornish cliff-castles was compiled by Cotton (1959); those of the Isle of Man, Wales, the Channel Islands and Brittany are represented in a few specific publications. There is therefore no complete corpus of promontory forts available for the whole Atlantic seaboard. The available information however is sufficient to indicate that multivallate promontory forts comparable with the Irish and Shetland examples, are rare, and are more characteristic of Brittany and Cornwall than of areas further north.

Windwick, the Landberg, Stoal and Hog Island Sound, together with the other specimens mentioned in the preceding section, are what Cotton (1959) describes as "simple", as opposed to "complex", multivallate forts. In the "simple" multivallate type, the design of the fort is a unity, the ramparts appearing to be of contemporary build; the "complex" multivallate fort has defences which appear to be of more than one period, usually being widely spaced, and the result is a series of separate barriers. It is the "simple" type, in which multivallation appears as a deliberate concept, rather than the "complex" form which is multivallate by chance rather than design, which concerns us here.

The British expedition of 1939 (Murray Threipland 1943) remains the main source of information on a selection of Breton forts. Most interesting among these is the Camp du César at Kervedan in the Ile de Groix, a fort of rather less than one hectare. It had two or perhaps three periods, but the main shaping of the defences belonged to the earliest—a large inner rampart and ditch, with six small low banks ranged in front of it. Murray Threipland believed that the fort at Pointe du Vieux Château, Belle-Ile-en-Mer, originally had a similar layout, although the Iron Age defences were obscured by mediaeval works. She considered that the scheme had been adopted because of the hard rock of the sites, "six small banks being as effective a protection against slingshot as three larger ones, and less trouble to construct". The main rampart at Camp du César certainly, and at Belle-Ile probably, was made of "a layer of turves holding in place a mass of rock debris, and retained on both sides by stone walls"; it is stated that there was neither "murus-gallicus" construction nor the stepped type of rampart found at Gurnards Head in Cornwall and Kercaradec in Brittany. The small outer banks were simple dumps. Doon Eask in County Kerry (Westropp 1910, 281; fig. 21) had a similar scheme; it is a spectacularly high headland guarded by "three rock-cut fosses separated by banks" with an inner defence of a stone-faced rampart. Cahercarberymore (ibid., 125; fig. 22) is a unique variant with two inner walls; it is built on a promontory with a natural step in it, the two walls being above the step, below it a series of low banks and ditches. In these

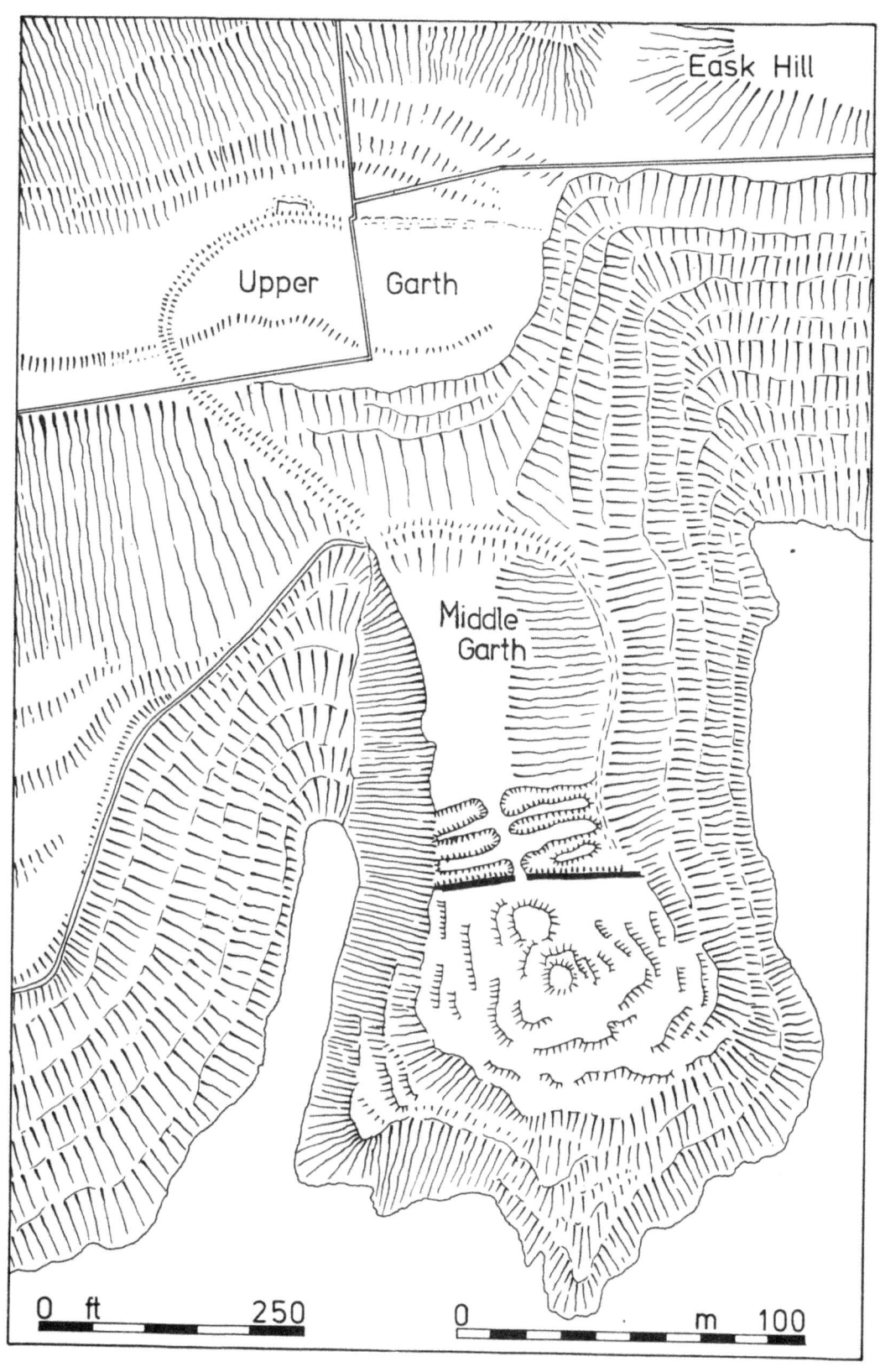

Fig. 21 Doon Eask, Co. Kerry, after Westropp (1910)

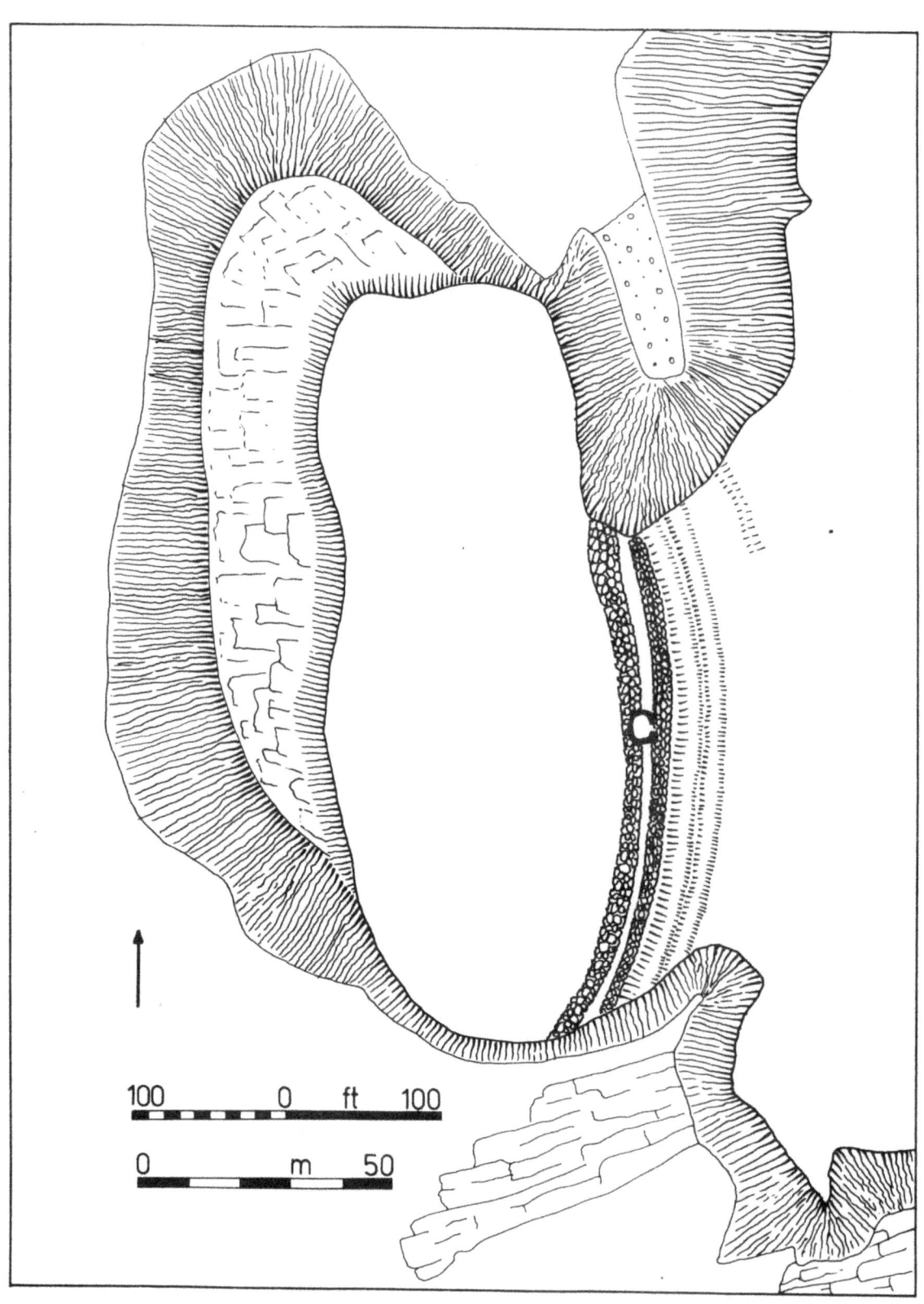

Fig. 22 Cahercarberymore, Co. Kerry, after Westropp (1910)

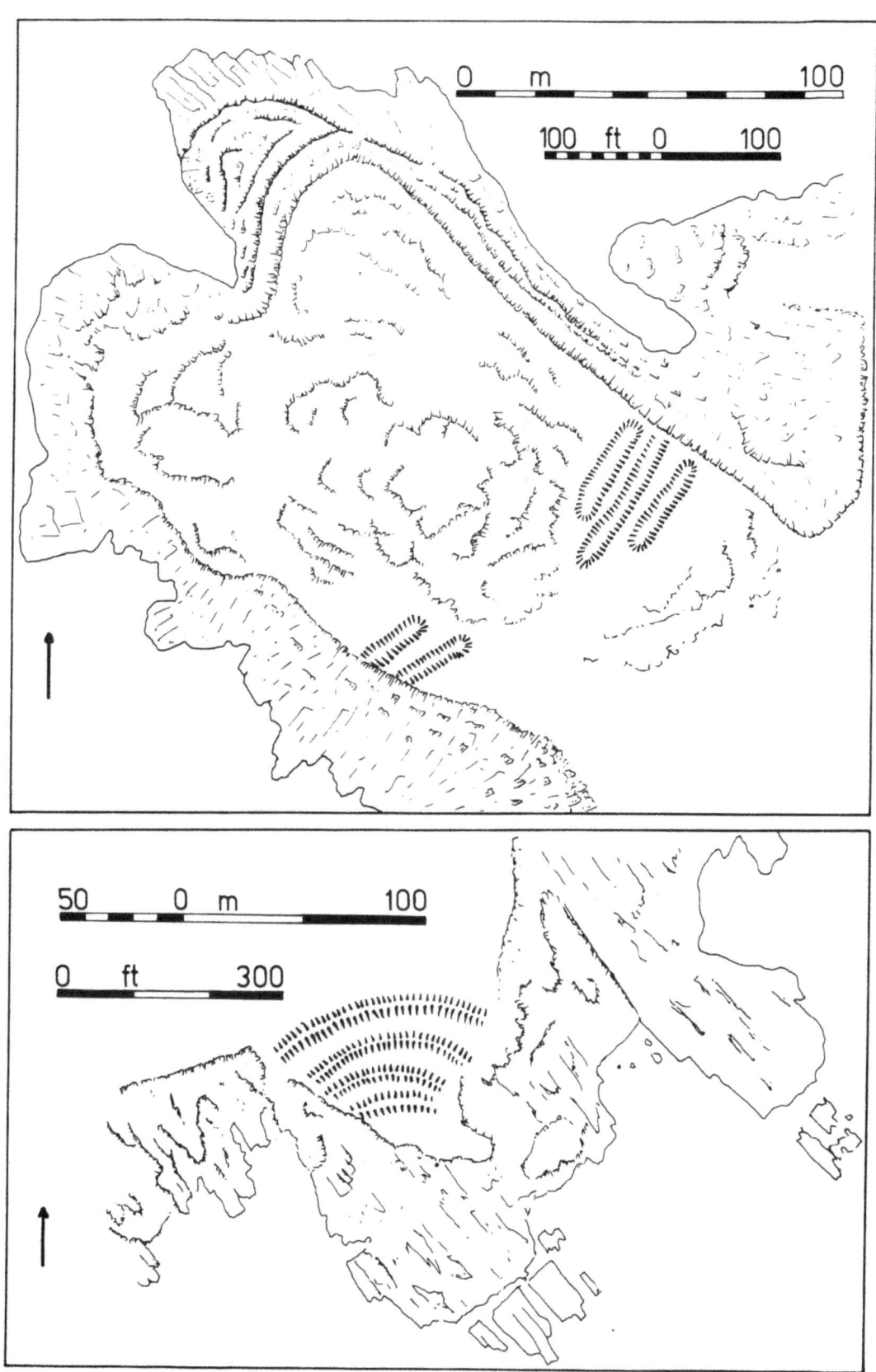

Fig. 23 Cornish cliff-castles: (above) St. Just in Penwith, Kenidjack Castle (below) Scilly, Giants Castle. Based on plans in Victoria County History of Cornwall (1907)

Irish and Breton sites, the problem of building a multivallate fort on intractable rock is solved in the same way as at the Landberg and Hog Island Sound; there are outer defences of inconsiderable dump banks overlooked by a substantial wall rampart.

Multivallate forts with three or more large unrevetted banks of more or less equal size, the style of Windwick or Stoal, also are rare. The biggest groups, each numbering four, are in Cornwall—Castle Kenidjack, Penwith; Giants' Castle, Scilly (fig. 23); Rumps Point, St Minver; and Gurnards Head; and in Galloway. Kirklaughlane in Wigtownshire (RCAMS 1912, 161, no. 431) is a classic example of three ramparts with external ditches, the ramparts increasing in height inwards. The innermost rampart stand about 2.6 m above the bottom of its ditch. Kenmuir Graves (RCAMS 1912, 150, no. 430) has the unusual arrangement of three ramparts and ditches on the inner sides, and a fourth innermost ditch. Borness Batteries (RCAMS 1914, 44, no. 60) has three crescentic ramparts with external ditches, and an entrance gap running straight through at the mid point. Kemps Walk (RCAMS 1912, 68, no. 174) has three ramparts of equal height, with external ditches. Ireland appears to be without comparable examples having three or more ramparts—none appear in the comprehensive publications of Westropp—although there are a few bivallate forts similar in construction, such as Doon Point and Doonabinnia in Co. Kerry (Westropp 1910, 208-11).

The picture, then is that multivallate coastal promontory forts are very widely and thinly scattered throughout the Atlantic promontory fort areas. The small number and wide spacing of these forts in Orkney and Shetland is compatible with this scanty overall distribution. The question is, does this mean that a cultural link existed across this wide area? The long-established idea, was that multivallate fortifications were developed in response to sling warfare, and that their distribution reflects a spread of the use of the sling.

The Northern multivallate forts of the "three-and-one" pattern do appear to be designed for defence with missile weapons. Their low outer banks are mere encumberances, capable of impeding an enemy's approach but not of shutting him out completely; they make sense only in relation to the more substantial rampart which overlooked them. Missiles launched from the top of this rampart should be particularly effective against an enemy scrambling over the outer banks, particularly as the defenders stationed at a greater height, should enjoy an advantage of missile range. It is unlikely however that the sling was the missile weapon behind the design of the Landberg, Hog Island Sound and Castle of Burwick. At all these forts the overall width of the defended zone is less than 30 m, while Wheeler (1943, 50-1) postulated a range of at least 100 yards (90 m) for effective slingshot. The approaching slingers therefore would have been able to retaliate against the defenders from a point not far short of 90 m from the main rampart (the height-advantage enjoyed by the defenders being only of the order of 7-10 m) up to the 30 m-point where the obstacle banks begin. On a promontory which narrows as the defences are approached, a numerically strong enemy would be able to concentrate his slingshot against the defenders on the shorter length of the main rampart, whose own outward fire would be dispersed and less effective. We cannot therefore accept that sling warfare was the design factor behind the "three-and-one" forts; it is more likely that the 30 m defended zone represents the extreme range of stones hurled by hand from the rampart. At the forts like Stoal and Windwick where all the ramparts stand at the same height, it is hard to contemplate any form of missile defence.

In Ireland, Doon Eask has a width of defended zone of 30 m, while at Cahercarberymore it is considerably less. At Borness Batteries in Galloway it is 20 m, at Kenmuir Graves within 30 m. In Cornwall, the defences of St. Just in Penwith are 30 m wide, but those of the Giants' Castle in Scilly are exceptional in covering 65 m. Defences covering a zone substantially narrower than the putative sling-range of 90 m are not therefore confined to the North; and we cannot claim a connection between multivallation and slinging, as far as promontory forts are concerned.

The association between multiple-bank systems and the introduction of sling warfare, in any event has been weakened along with the old watertight division between forts with univallate wall defences and those with multivallate dumps. The important excavation report (Avery Sutton and Banks 1967) on Rainsborough in Northamptonshire, which proved to be a bivallate fort with two wall-defences, focussed attention on what had been an over-simplification. Rainsborough's ramparts also proved to be constructed in steps or terraces; the occurrence of this feature in a fifth-century B.C. context deep in the Midland Shires, was a corrective to the long-held belief that terraced ramparts were a characteristic of the Atlantic seaboard and evidence of seaborne contacts. They had been found at Gurnards Head in Cornwall (Gordon 1941), Portadoona and Carrigillihy in Co. Cork (O'Kelly 1952), and Kercaradec in Brittany (Wheeler 1957). These terraced ramparts, like coastal promontory forts in general, had been linked with the maritime Gaulish tribe named by Caesar as the Veneti.

The cliff-castles of Cornwall and Brittany so often have been called Venetic (Cotton 1961, 107) that the real implications of the literary material on which the association is based, have been overlooked. The Veneti are known from Caesar as a vigorous seafaring and trading people, and it has been convenient to see them as the agent of diffusion of cultural traits from Brittany to Cornwall and up the Irish Sea. Caesar (De Bello Gallico III, 12-14) does make clear that the main oppida of the Veneti were coastal, but equally that they were not cliff-castles. These strongholds had to be approached across tidal reefs which made access on foot difficult, and also hindered shipping: "(oppida) posita in extremis lingulis promunturiisque neque pedibus aditum haberent, cum ex alto se aestus incitavisset, ... neque navibus, quod rursus se minuente aestu naves in vadis afflictarentur". Attacking such a position demanded major works of engineering, building a causeway across the tidal zone, then banking it up as a ramp against the walls: "extruso mari aggere ac molibus atque his oppidi moenibus adaequatis". Since Caesar was too practical a general to have attempted to build his way "aggere ac molibus" up a fifty-metre cliff, we may assume that the Venetic oppidum was no cliff-castle but a low-lying tidal island fortress such as the Ile Istilec, Sauzon (Bernier 1963) which at over 3 ha comes closer to "oppidum" size. Caesar operating without naval support was annoyed to find the Veneti, hard pressed in their strongholds, invariably escaping by sea: which implies that these oppida had some access by boat. Finally, "duck-stamped" pottery, long thought to be a Venetic export from Brittany, has been shown by Peacock (1968) to originate in the Malvern Hills.

Having eliminated the Veneti—at any rate until there is positive evidence of their involvement—how far are we justified in treating the Brittany-Cornwall-Irish Sea area as one of cultural interchange in the Early Iron Age? The duck-stamped ware is a very tangible evidence of trade, although it is taking place in the reverse direction from that originally envisaged by archaeologists. The promontory forts of the cliff-coasts indeed are remarkably similar. The sea is an open highway unless it is deliberately closed by some strong naval power, so it is more realistic to assume that trading contacts took place, than that they did not. But it matters more, whether such contacts were significant in broad historical terms. And if we do admit that Brittany, Cornwall and the Irish Sea coasts as far north as Galloway, are a region within which significant cultural interchange took place, must we accept also that this region extends all the way to Shetland where we find cliff-castles more Cornish-looking than many in Brittany, Galloway or Ireland?

*   *   *   *   *

Atlantic contacts between northern and western Scotland, and south-western England, have of course been proposed without any reference to promontory forts. Childe, by no means a hyper-diffusionist, was convinced that it was a straightforward case of culture-transmission from the South-West of England to the Atlantic provinces of Scotland; he based his arguments on small-artefact assemblages, relying heavily on those from Glastonbury, and on the stone round-house plans (Childe 1935 and 1940). He was prepared to state categorically that "the south-western origin of the broch culture remains an archaeological fact", and used this as a parallel for the spread of the megalithic religion to the north two millennia earlier. Childe's statements were elaborated by Sir Lindsay Scott in 1947 and 1948; Scott associated the emigration from southern England into northern Scotland, with the political situation during the decades preceding the Claudian invasion of Britain. He went considerably further than Childe in the analysis of material culture, in particular deriving the decorative motifs on Hebridean pottery from the south-west; but found difficulty in sustaining the parallel, and was thrown back on admitting that "the pottery style which the colonists derived from the south-western cultures suffered a rapid degeneration". He saw his immigration in terms of "the conditions of unrest which developed in the mid first century B.C. and continued into the first century A.D., as a result of Caesar's conquest of Gaul, the emigration of Armorican tribes to Britain" (the Veneti !), "the western advance of the Belgae in England, and finally the Claudian conquest of Britain." The postulated settlement was north to the Hebrides with colonisation there, then around Cape Wrath, by-passing the inhospitable coasts of Wester Ross and Sutherland, eventually to the islands around Scapa Flow. It then divided into two, one branch going north through the North Isles of Orkney and on to Shetland, the other petering out in a southward movement along the lowland coast of Caithness. Scott of course held the view that very few of the brochs had been tower-like, and thought that in origin they were not forts, but a development of the round-house tradition ultimately of south-western origin. His dating of the migration from the south resulted in a late date for the brochs, which he did not consider to be earlier than the early second century A.D.

The most notable recent advocate of the diffusionist view has been Dr. E. W. MacKie, whose important paper of 1965 set out in clear terms the chronological relationship between brochs and wheelhouses, and left no doubt that the brochs derive from a fort tradition quite separate from that of round-house building. But in looking for parallels in artefact assemblages between Scotland and south-western England—in this case Wessex—his methods and Scott's are essentially similar. MacKie's thesis is based on certain classes of objects supposedly common to the two areas—bead-rimmed pottery, spiral finger-rings, parallelopiped bone dice, and rotary querns. He used the negative evidence of the absence from the Hebrides of ring-headed pins of types common in Wessex, to tie down the period of immigration to the first century B.C. He claimed that the "guard-chambers" of brochs were derived from those of South British hillforts. Using this evidence he has proposed an immigration from Wessex at a time of Belgic expansion into that area, $\underline{c}$. 80-70 B.C., of "Iron Age B families there who could not bear the decline in status which must have accompanied the arrival of powerful new tribes" (MacKie 1969b, 56-9).

Detailed objections against MacKie's thesis have been laid by D. V. Clarke of the National Museum of Antiquities, Edinburgh, in papers published in 1970 and 1971. He has suggested that the bone dice in the North all belong to the early centuries A.D., that is at least a hundred years after they had gone out of use in southern Britain. Spiral rings seem to have had a very wide time span and to have "enjoyed several periods of popularity, without any one period providing a major impulse to another". The evidence of the bead-rimmed pottery depends too heavily on one isolated find from Dun Mor Vaul. Clarke points out that the examples of guard-chambers in English hillforts seem all to be much earlier than the broch period. In the view of the present writer, as noted in the previous chapter, the mural cells of brochs have no defensive function and are not comparable with the guardrooms behind the gateways of English hillforts. Of all the material links suggested by MacKie, we are left only with the rotary querns, which somehow must have been introduced from outside. They are very common finds in brochs, although in nearly all cases they probably belong to wheelhouse rather than to broch levels; invariably they are of the flat disc form with upright handle which in Curwen's classic study (1937) is derived from the bun-shaped ones in use in southern Scotland in the early centuries A.D. According to Curwen their eventual appearance in wheelhouses would be due to a gradual drift northwards. At Dun Mor Vaul however (MacKie 1974, 138) flat disc querns were found in pre-broch and broch construction levels, well within the first century B.C.; these showed no signs of recent derivation from the bun-shaped forms. The querns therefore may be an instance of direct introduction from southern England into Scotland.

But on the overall matter of the diffusionist explanation of the origin of the broch culture, the state of our knowledge of Iron Age structures in the Highlands and Islands still demands the cautious approach of Clarke, who sensibly questions the validity of conclusions drawn from the distribution of small objects very thinly scattered over wide areas. He recommends (1970) that the whole matter of Atlantic Scotland—Wessex contacts be put aside until more comprehensive evidence is available. "The lack of sufficient stratigraphically excavated sites has hindered, and will continue to hinder, the interpretation of the complex cultural sequence in the Atlantic province. In the absence of such a sequence, with well defined types, it is perhaps too early to search for origins". Rotary querns and multivallate promontory forts are not, as yet, an adequate foundation on which to erect a structure of theory about the origins of brochs. As we shall see from a brief examination of the Northern multivallate broch-outworks, the multivallate tradition seems to exist, probably slightly pre-dating, and certainly continuing alongside, the developed broch tradition; and there is no evidence that any intrusive tradition which the multivallate forts represent, contributed significantly to the attainment of architectural perfection of the broch towers.

That multivallate fort-building is not native to the North is however highly probable. The multiple dump-rampart construction is grossly unsuited to the geology of the area. At Hog Island Sound especially, the soil is so thin, the bedrock so close to the surface, that the builders have had to scratch material from wide areas to create an extraordinarily feeble set of dump banks. The use of traditional stone or turf techniques would have enabled an effective fortification to be built with much less trouble. But so little is known about multivallate cliff-castles in the Irish Sea area, Cornwall and Brittany, that even after the comprehensive excavation of a northern fort—the Landberg appears to offer the best intact deposits—we should be no nearer understanding the reality of any north-south links.

* * * * *

If we postulate maritime contact operating along Britain's Atlantic seaboard, the distribution of promontory forts from Cornwall to Galloway fits the assumption nicely. The discovery of matching forts, most readily explicable as products of outside influence, in Orkney and Shetland, would extend that seaway to the maximum length possible before the discovery and colonisation of Faeroe and Iceland in Early Christian and Viking times gave Britain in general, and the Northern Isles in particular, a place within a much wider North Atlantic network. But the absence of multivallate forts from the Hebrides is puzzling. In a boat of course it is possible to pass in a few days or weeks the length of the west coast of Scotland, without ever stopping for long enough to leave one's mark on the archaeological record; and there may have been some political reason why travellers moving, say, between the Orkneys and the Irish Sea, had more effective contacts with the communities at the extremities of the voyage than with those they met in the middle. At the present state of knowledge, we can barely guess at what may have happened. It is a fact that multivallate forts have not been found

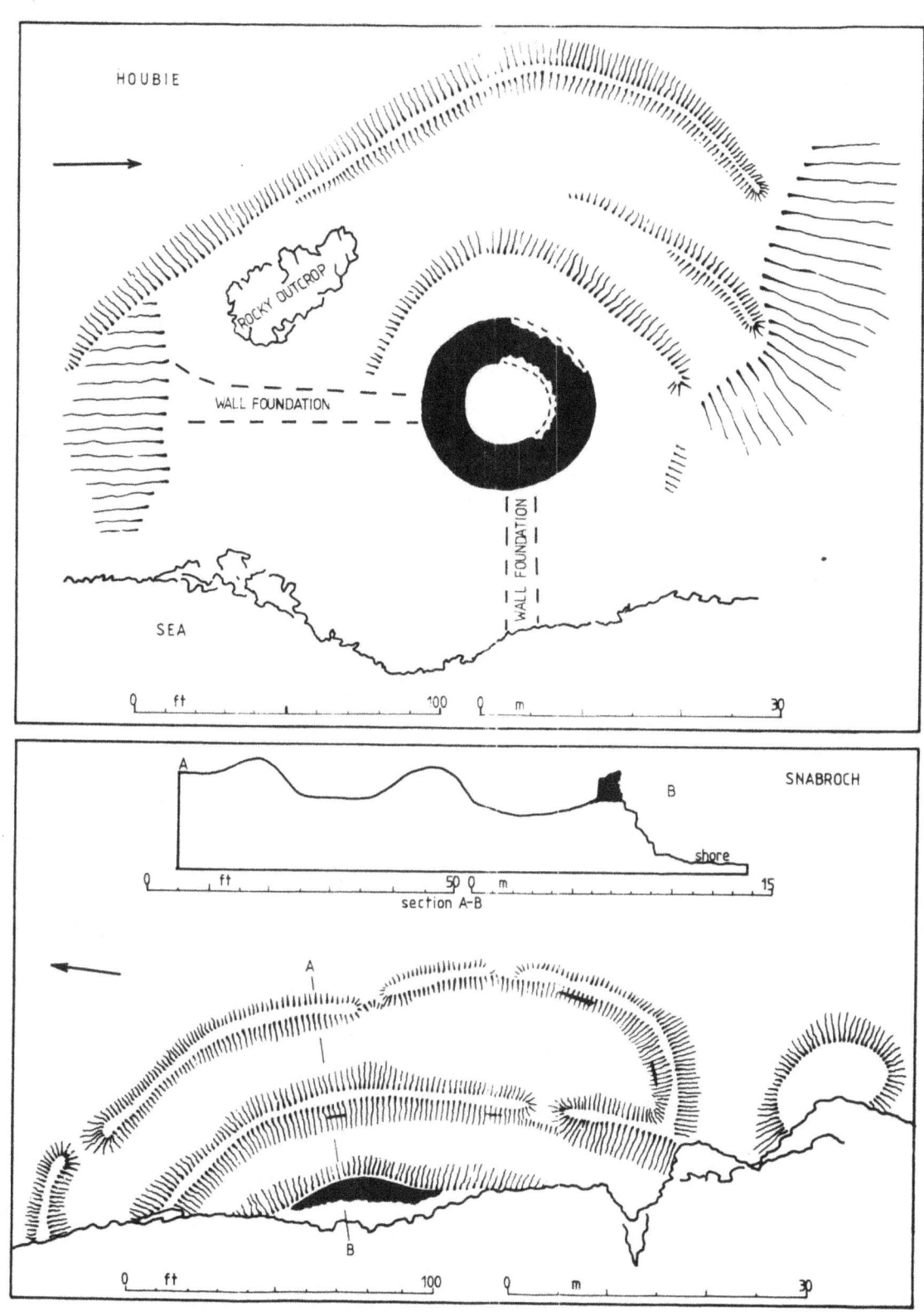

Fig. 24 Fetlar, Shetland, brochs with multiple outworks (above) Houbie (below) Snabroch. RCAMS plans by C. S. T. Calder

in the Hebrides and that complicated systems of broch-outworks, which are a notable feature of Orkney and Shetland, do not occur there either.

Whether the multivallate fortifications normally pre-date the brochs within them, as does the ring-wall at Clickhimin, is a question we cannot yet answer. That multivallate promontory forts do exist separate from brochs might be taken to suggest that they are earlier than brochs; but this is not conclusive. Multiple bank-and-ditch defences complement a broch in a way that a massive structure like the Midhowe forework does not. The Midhowe forework, being a near-vertical structure close up against the broch, is tactically unsatisfactory—once taken, it would give cover to an attacker—and makes more sense if we envisage it standing by itself before the broch was added. The multivallate systems protecting the brochs of Burland or Houbie are much more logically related to the towers, which of course is not proof of contemporaneity.

At Snabroch and Houbie (fig. 24), both in Fetlar, Shetland, the fortifications are built against the edge of a straight section of coast. Houbie has a broch on the summit of a rocky knoll, protected by steep slopes and two banks. Snabroch is a puzzling site where the central fortification survives only as a fragment on the very edge of the shore; it is usually called a broch, but the surviving masonry is not a segment of a regular circle. Protecting it are two banks separated by a broad and deep ditch. At Burland (fig. 20), a precipitous promontory 7 km south of Lerwick, a well-preserved broch is so arranged that its doorway opens on to a narrow path above the brink. To landward it is protected by three lines of defence with a central entrance gap running straight through at the middle point. The outer line is a rampart of loose material with a revetment of stonework on both sides; it resembles the outer defence to the Ness of Burgi blockhouse. The middle line is a dump bank and is less substantial, while the inner one to the east of the path also is a dump. On the west side however its place is taken by a very neatly-built wall, with a well-finished end-face set slightly back from the cliff-edge, which reflects the blockhouse concept and presumably is meant to serve the same purpose as the blockhouses. At Burland then, we appear to have the multivallate tradition combining with the blockhouse idea.

IV

THE MEANING OF FORTS AND BROCHS

That brochs were serious fortifications is no longer in doubt; who built them, and why, we still do not know. There must have been some special political situation which caused large numbers of these cleverly engineered and highly expensive fortresses to be built within, it appears, quite a limited period. Whatever this political situation was, it quickly passed away, for wherever there is archaeological evidence, we find that although the sites remained in occupation, the military capability was done away with.

This last point is the least doubtful fact in the broch story. At some time not long after reaching their fullest development, the brochs were superseded by undefended settlements. Wheelhouses and (in Orkney especially) slab-structures were built in and around the towers, which were partly demolished either to provide material or to remove the danger from falling masonry. At Jarlshof, the upper part of the tower either fell or was taken down during the wheelhouse period (Hamilton 1956, 68). The broch of Oxtro by Early Christian times had been reduced to a mound, and this was used as a burial tumulus for inserted short cists (Petrie 1890, 76-80). At Gurness and Midhowe, the slab-structures which engulfed broch and outworks, destroyed the defensibility of the sites, and the same can be seen to have happened at Borwick where a hut is cut right through the massive forework. MacKie (1971) has cleverly demonstrated that the demolition of the Keiss South broch, in Caithness, came very early in the archaeological sequence. Very few brochs were left to survive to anything like their original height. That this situation had developed in antiquity, and not during recent centuries of stone-robbing, is strongly suggested by the appearance of Mousa in ch. 33 of Egils Saga and ch. 93 of Orkneyinga Saga. Mousa is the only broch recognizable as such, to appear in the sagas, and that it does so in two of them, confirms that even by Norse times its survival was exceptional.

What situation had engendered the flurry of broch-building is still a matter of argument. It is not even agreed whether brochs are the strongholds of an aggressive conquering aristocracy or the bolt-holes of a frightened and peace-loving peasant population. On the face of it, no fortification would appear to have been more passive in defence than a broch tower. It had no opening except one low and narrow doorway, the door being set so far back in the passage that the ram could not be used against it. The wall was too high to be climbed without difficulty and its weight gave the stones such cohesion that they could not be prised out or battered down. The inhabitants could have done little more than barricade themselves inside and wait until the attacker recognized the stalemate and went away. The only active defensive measure necessary, would have been to crouch behind the top parapet and drop stones on anyone who did try to clamber up. The only serious danger to a broch was fire; even a fifteen-metre wall would not keep out all incendiary missiles, and the internal timbering and the kiln-like shape made the broch a first-rate furnace. Signs of violent heat are clearly to be seen on the inside walls of Borwick and Crosskirk.

This picture may be entirely misleading. The Norman conquering aristocracy in England built tower-keeps such as Rochester and Hedingham, which are as solidly passive as any broch. The most aggressive of warlords may be glad of an invulnerable redoubt safe from surprise attack, which can be held by a handful of men while the main warband is away. The direct comparison between mediaeval castle and broch was expressed very forcibly by Simpson (1954); "the brochs were not erected to defend the countryside against invaders, but were the strongholds of a conquering aristocracy securing themselves against the native population whom they had enslaved, and doubtless also against their neighbours in the internecine conflicts against each other, like the feudal barons of later times". So far from being an architecture of fear, suggests Simpson, the brochs were built to dominate; his paper remains one of the most cogent contributions to the broch discussion.

Whether it was haughty aristocrats or frightened peasants who built the towers, the concentrated investment of manpower must have been enormous. The society which produced brochs therefore was highly organised and the aristocratic structure is perhaps the easier to envisage. The supervision of building operations doubtless was entrusted to specialists who took their consultancy services from site to site—an itinerant technician class of highly professional engineers. Although many of the essential elements of broch architecture had been current in the Northern blockhouses and the Western semibrochs, the difference between these comparitively modest structures and the brochs is a major one, and there is as yet no obvious line of evolution. Simpson's (1954, 35) view is that "the broch design remains so standardised as to prompt the suggestion, put forward by more than one investigator, that the conception was a single one, evolved in the mind of some highly gifted master of construction. Such an idea is perhaps somewhat hard of acceptance in these modern days, when the dogmas of evolution and typological development have been pushed to a point where there is little room left for the individual genius thinking out something new on his own. Yet the history of military invention during two world wars may well inspire us with a different view". The pupils of such an inventor would have formed an elite school of architecture, commanding high prices for the application of their technology.

If Simpson is right in comparing the broch and its outworks with the mediaeval keep and bailey, should we assume a comparable level of manning for defence? The broch itself, like the keep, could have been held by a dozen men; but the defence of outworks would have needed far larger numbers and more aggressive measures of defence. This also applies to promontory forts, most notably to the multivallate forts of the "three-and-one" design; the banks barring the approach to the Landberg or Hog Island Sound are slight obstacles, effective only in conjunction with a hail of stones from the top of the rampart. The Landberg, in terms of area, is a very small fort which cannot have sheltered many families; the manpower available to defend it would have been small, but as the promontory is narrow, the length of defence-line is manageable. At Hog Island Sound the defences run across a much wider approach, but how wide was the former rock-bridge cannot be known.

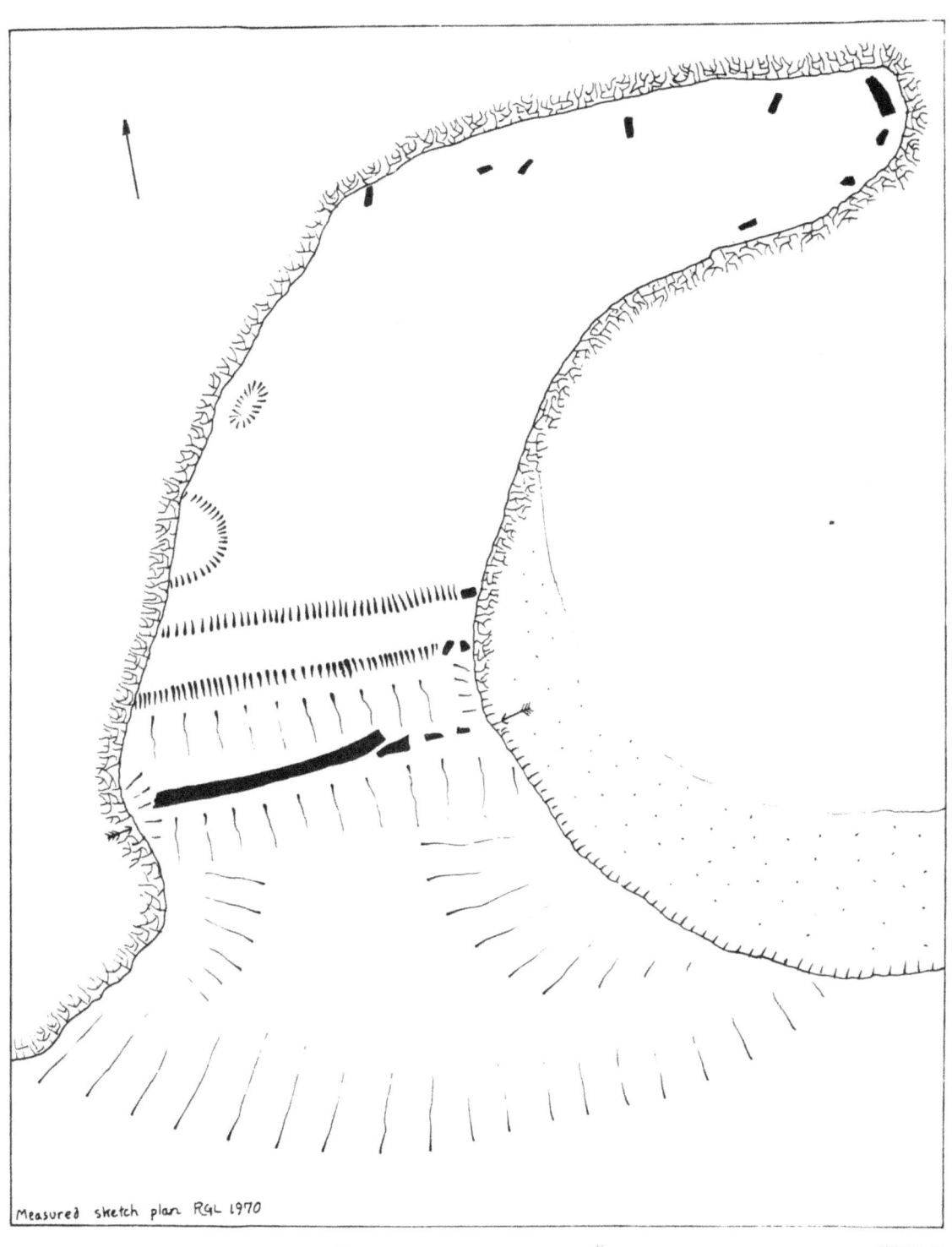

Fig. 25 Castle of Sand Geo, Copinsay, Orkney, sketch plan. The width of the isthmus, measured along line of wall between arrows, is 9 m

If a position is seriously meant to be defensible, the inherent strength of the fortification itself must be made greater as the manpower available to defend it is decreased. Thus the broch of Mousa could be defended by very few, while a multivallate promontory fort needed far more active defence but at any rate had room for more men. There is however a class of promontory forts which we may call "small strengths" where an apparently weak fortification is used to protect a very restricted area. The narrow promontory pierced by a natural arch at Gote o'Tram, near Wick in Caithness, is cut off by a U-sectioned rock-cut ditch with remains of a bank on its inner lip. The very considerable effort which went into the rock-cutting, implies that the site is at least intended to be a fort. Another small weakly-defended site occurs on the cliff-coast north-west from Burgh Head on Stronsay, Orkney, and an example very similar to this is illustrated in fig. 25, pl. 20, at Castle of Sand Geo, Copinsay, Orkney. It is difficult to imagine that such insignificant sites could have contained the manpower necessary to defend them.

Remembering the utter military nonsense of the blockhouse forts, particularly Burgi Geos; the quirkish asymmetrical layout of banks at Windwick and the Landberg; the determination to have dump banks at the Landberg and Hog Island Sound where hard rock made it nearly impossible to dig the ditches and get the dump material; the tactical absurdity of having successive lines of defence standing at the same level, as do the ramparts of Stoal and Windwick; and now the merely token fortifying of the small strengths: we are driven to the conclusion that the builders of all these forts were more concerned about status than with serious defence. Although the brochs too must have been status-symbols, the more effective as such the higher they were built, brochs were a very effective defence, which Burgi Geos, for all its eyrie-like siting, was not seriously designed to be.

There are other promontory forts of individualistic design, which do not fall into recognizable categories and the date and function of which could only be determined by excavations. A few, such as the Brough of Bigging (fig. 7) have been heavily damaged by erosion and stone-robbing so that their original form is difficult to discover. Bigging has a single low bank on the inner lip of a natural rift which cuts across a broad promontory; 30 m further seaward, where the isthmus becomes higher and narrower, are confused remains of other defences consisting of indeterminate stone-revetted earthworks. At the Brough of Deerness on the far side of Orkney Mainland, the massive "vallum monasterii" of a mediaeval monastery, may well be in origin an Iron Age fort; as indeed was suggested by the perspicacious George Low in 1774 (Low 1879, 55). But little can be said about these sites without excavation. The remarkable fort at Brough Ness of Garth, Sandness, Shetland, is so peculiar that one wonders if it does not belong to some other period-context than the Early Iron Age. It is a peninsula separated from the mainland by a storm-beach; the slope from the beach to the promontory is defended by two terrace-walls built against the slope, with the tumbled remains of a third wall on the crest (Fig. 16 pl. 21-22). All these walls are crudely built of rounded beach-boulders. Within the defences are three circular houses, about 3 m in diameter, and two oblong ones, with remarkably straight sides and rounded corners, 6 m long internally, one complete and the others partly gone over the cliff. These buildings are clustered behind the inner wall, and all are solidly built of stone. The general impression given by Brough Ness of Garth is that it is unlike anything else, and it would be idle to speculate who built it.

The blockhouse forts were ascribed by Hamilton to conquering invaders. Heavy immigrations from south-western England into Atlantic Scotland were seen by Childe, Scott and MacKie as the origin of the broch culture itself; the multivallate forts, had these been known to the earlier writers, might well have been claimed as supporting evidence. In fact, it is unlikely that any promontory forts in the Northern Isles have a direct link with invasions, either as the invaders' bases of aggression or as the response of a defending population; for with the one exception of the Landberg, there is no convincing example of a strategically positioned fort. Scatness with its two blockhouses is hedged with reefs and guarded by the fearful tide-race which gave the name Dunrossness to this extremity of Shetland-Dynröstarnes, the Ness of the Roaring Tide-Race. Huxter, isolated in its landlocked loch, just will not do as a strategic site, and neither will Clickhimin. And what invader would have established his base camp at Burgi Geos? Who would have selected such an extraordinary site as the rallying-point of resistance? What strategic value lies in the nondescript positions occupied by Windwick, Stoal, or Hog Island Sound? The Landberg admittedly dominates the two least rock-encumbered landing-places on Fair Isle, and commands the overland route leading from these to the habitable part of the island; and Fair Isle itself may have had a strategic value when boats were rowed and stages of voyages kept as short as possible (this would not apply to sailing vessels, for which Fair Isle is a death-trap). But this one apparently strategic fort among so many, may be fortuitous; it may just have happened to be the right sort of promontory to build a fort on. The conclusion must be, that any political significance these sites possessed, lay within temporary political contexts within the island-groups themselves; to recover details of such passing historical situations is beyond the reach of archaeology.

The controversy over the origin and development of brochs looks like continuing for a long time to come. The diffusionist explanations of the spread of material culture direct from south-western England to the Hebrides, and of the spread of broch architecture from there to Caithness, Orkney and Shetland, are simplistic and unsatisfactory. Clarke's warnings against the use of small-object distributions, where the objects are thinly scattered over so wide an area, in our present state of knowledge must preclude acceptance of the Wessex origin of the broch culture. And the cleanness of the place-name record should convince us that no immigrant Celtic-speaking people ever dominated Orkney and Shetland. The ultimately Hebridean origin of brochs must always be suspect, in that it is curious that the roots of something so remarkable and vigorous, should lie outside the main area of perfection where brochs are most numerous. There is no need to doubt MacKie's belief in the semibrochs as Hebridean progenitors of broch architecture. But the straight linear progression, from semibrochs through Hebridean ground-galleried brochs to Northern solid-based brochs, is an over-simplification. In the open landscape of the islands linked by the free sea, it is unlikely to have happened that way. The Western Isles, Orkney and Shetland would have been subject to comings and goings in both directions; in an atmosphere of mutual awareness, sustained by maritime contact, brochs were developed and refined.

The Shetland blockhouses and the Hebridean semibrochs have their distinctive traits—cells in one, galleries in the other—but essentially they are similar structures. They are expressions of local individualism within the overall awareness. The processes by which these structures were transformed into towering brochs, are still unclear to us; Simpson's single mind of genius is probably the best explanation. The progression from ground-galleried to solid-based brochs is likely to be valid; but while the solid-based form is distinctively Northern, the ground-gallereied prototype is not exclusively Hebridean. There is a gallery in the Nybster forework. The broch of Midhowe, after a failure, was converted from a ground-galleried to a solid-based one. And what of Burraland—surely an obvious "galleried dun" if only it were not in Shetland and therefore automatically called a broch? Very few Shetland and Orkney brochs are sufficiently clear of debris for us to be sure that they do not contain basal galleries.

A seaway is open to all comers unless a strong naval power deliberately closes it. That is a difficult and expensive thing to do and sustain. It is unlikely that any such naval power was effective against the western seaways in prehistoric times. The Northern Isles are naturally open: General Wade did not need to open them up as he had to do to the Highlands after the 1745 rebellion. We need find no difficulty in imagining contact between the Hebrides and the Northern Isles during the development period of broch architecture. It is certain that throughout history there have been adventurers, at least, who have made long voyages. Such a distant contact is revealed by the chevaux-de-frise at Burgi Geos. Contacts as far south as the Irish Sea and possibly beyond, are strongly suggested by the multivallate forts. But Burgi Geos is unique and multivallate promontory forts are few. They prove what we may reasonably expect, that there was the occasional long voyage or chance chain of contacts. They are not enough to prove that such occasional voyages or contacts far way to the South, had a major effect on cultural development in the North. They may explain the multivallate forts but they do not mean that the development of brochs was owed to massive immigrations of Celtic or other peoples. The promontory forts do suggest far-flung contacts but it is not indicated that these contacts had a lasting effect on the historical development of Orkney and Shetland.

APPENDIX 1

GAZETTEER

This Gazetteer includes all sites in Shetland and Orkney and on the northern coast of Scotland, which in the writer's opinion are certainly or probably Iron Age promontory forts. Not all of these are mentioned in the text; only those which are discussed there, are marked on the maps (figs. 2 and 3). References are given to published works where these exist. In some cases the only source is the Ordnance Survey's archaeological card index, which is available for consultation by arrangement. At time of writing, the main copy of this is housed in the Ordnance Survey's premises at 43, Rose Street, Edinburgh.

SUTHERLAND

Eilean nan Caorach, Durness.
National Grid reference NC 350716.

A large rocky plateau projecting from an entirely deserted coast, is surrounded on three sides by sea cliffs, and to landward slopes down very steeply to a broad isthmus. A wide track climbs diagonally up the slope from the E, being supported near the bottom on built terracing of large boulders. Along the top of the slope is a wall, its foundation course being a line of massive boulders, many of which measure more than a metre each way. At the head of the track the wall is pierced by an entrance gap 2.5 m wide, lined with similar boulders. Behind the wall at its E end is a stone hut circle of 3.7 m overall diameter. There are numerous circular depressions on the summit, but as the site lies within a naval firing range most if not all of them may be shell-holes. The more portable stones have been removed from the wall to build shelters for sheep.

Seanachaisteal, Durness.
National Grid reference NC 406679

The site is a promontory with sheer cliffs on the W side but only a moderately steep slope down to rocks and the sea on the E. It rises to a limestone knoll which to the rear is protected by crags about 6 m high which fall to a terrace a few metres wide above the sea cliffs. There are traces of a parapet along the land-facing edge of the knoll, and on the summit against the crag is a horseshoe-shaped depression which may be a hut foundation. In front of the knoll is a very broad and stony rampart. As all the ground is hummocky, it is difficult to identify the limits of the rampart material but the width seems to be around 10 m. There is a considerable hollow in

the summit just N of the centrally-placed entrance gap, which has no distinctive features although its position is clear enough. Below the rampart is a wide, flat-bottomed ditch.
RCAMS 1911b, 54, no. 158.

Dun Mhairtein, Baligill, Farr
National Grid Reference NC 854664

A promontory about 27 m high projects from the cliffs 200 m NNE of the crofting township of Baligill. It curves westwards so as to run almost parallel with the mainland, from which it is separated by a deep geo; the fortification cuts across the tail of the promontory, enclosing an area about 22m x 24 m. The fort is overlooked by the higher cliffs on the mainland side of the geo. The main feature is a stone-revetted rampart varying between 4.9 and 5.8 m in thickness and up to 1.8 m high, pierced slightly E of centre by an entrance gap 1.02 m wide at the outer end and widening inwards. There is a doorcheck formed by an upright slab at right angles to the E wall of the passage. Before the rampart the ground has been scooped back from either cliff-edge, leaving a 2.5 m-wide causeway in line with the entrance. On the W side only a bank, some 3.6 m thick and 3 m from the rampart, intervenes between the rampart and the scooped ditch, which on this side descends to the brink in three broad steps.

The fort interior contains a complex of structures forming a shapeless mound, within which the interior of a stone-built hut has recently been exposed, presumably by an amateur excavator; this is not mentioned in the Royal Commission Inventory, nor does it appear on the sketch-plan in the Ordnance Survey index. The hut is rectilinear, the excavator having cleared the whole 2.74 m length of one wall and portions of the adjoining walls; the rest of the interior is choked with debris. The building is very carefully constructed, the lower 0.9 m of the wall being of orthostats above which is preserved 0.3 m of good dry masonry, built of small flat pieces of quarried stone. At the SW corner where the masonry is preserved to the greatest height, the topmost courses oversail slightly, but this may just be due to bulging. In the debris one large stone is notable; it is 0.25 m square in cross-section and at least 1.2 m long, and seems deliberately shaped, perhaps as a pillar or lintel.

Some 3 m NW of the hut is a deep depression giving access to a souterrain-like tunnel which runs NE and downwards (following the ground slope) for 10.7 m, emerging on the cliff face. Although it is choked with debris to within 0.5 m of the roof, it is possible to see along the whole length of it. The roof is of heavy lintels on orthostats and dry walling, being broken in at a point 3 m from the entrance; in this area are many erect earthfast slabs.
RCAMS 1911b, 63, no. 191.
Ordnance Survey index ref. NC 86 NE 1.

CAITHNESS

Neck of Brough, Thurso
National Grid reference ND 060710

An L-shaped promontory curves around to lie parallel with the mainland, from which it is separated by a deep geo. Along the landward edge is a bank containing traces of drystone walling. The isthmus, which is lower, has been wave-scoured to the bare rock and no defensive features survive. No other structures are visible on the promontory.
RCAMS 1911a, 125, no. 454
Ordnance Survey index ref. ND 07 SE 1

Holborn Head, Thurso
National Grid reference ND 108715

The broad cliff-headland which encloses Thurso Bay on the NW has been cut into by the sea along faults, creating two long, parallel chasms which reduce the width of the isthmus to some 55 m. Immediately seaward of the inner of the two chasms there is a bank 0.75 m high, of loose material derived from a quarry-scoop behind it. There is then a stiff climp to the headland, crowned by a wall 0.5 m to 0.9 m high and 2.4 m broad, of small flat slabs with a facing of larger ones. The entrance gap, now featureless, was in the middle, opposite the approach between the heads of the chasms. Nothing else is visible on the promontory except for some erect earthfast slabs on the clifftop on the W side, immediately behind the rampart.
RCAMS 1911a, 120, no. 438

West Murkle, Thurso
National Grid reference ND 158699

At the head of the bay of Haven, immediately opposite the end of the cart-track past the farm of West Murkle, is a grassy hillock forming a blunt headland some 6 m above high-water level. Around it runs a considerable bank and ditch which start in a straight line from the cliff on the E side, but about half-way across curve sharply W and seawards. The top of the bank stands some 3 m above the bottom of the U-sectioned ditch; the bank has a core of large stones and probably a masonry revetment. A slight depression about midway along the bank is probably not the original entrance, which possibly was at one of the ends lost by erosion. Within the fort, nothing is visible on the ground except for a few erect slabs behind the rampart at the E end. In the cliff-sections however portions of walls can be seen, suggesting that the defended area, which is thickly overgrown, was quite densely built-up.
RCAMS 1911a, 125, no. 451

St. Johns Point, Canisbay
National Grid reference ND 310751

The broad cliff-promontory is cut off by a massive rampart about 3 m high, fronted by a U-sectioned ditch some 15 m wide. The entrance may be represented by a gap towards the W end, but this is not certain. A modern drystone dyke runs along the top of the rampart. No structures are visible on the 4-hectare area of rough grazing which the rampart encloses, but against its rear is a rectangular building, the exterior of which is buried, the interior clear to a depth of 0.6 m but full of nettles. The interior measurement is 7 m x 3 m. It is constructed of good dry masonry. Curle (RCAMS) who gives it a length of 32 feet (9.75 m), which presumably is the exterior length, says that "in the interior two slabs protrude, which may have formed the ends of a long cist". The building is said locally to be a chapel.
RCAMS 1911a, pp. 17 and 20, nos. 40 and 56

Skirza Head broch, Canisbay
National Grid reference ND 395684

This was one of the many brochs excavated at the turn of the century by Sir Francis Tress Barry. It stands on a cliff-promontory defended by a broad artificial ditch with a low rampart inside of it. On the S side immediately outside the ditch is a setting of erect slabs. Curle (RCAMS) reported these as covering an area 25 feet x 6 feet (7.62 m x 1.83 m), appearing to be "the remains of four rows roughly set in alignment some 3 feet to 4 feet (0.91 m to 1.22 m) apart". The stones themselves were 1 foot to 2 feet (0.31 m to 0.61 m) high and set 2 feet 5 inches (0.74 m) to 4 feet (1.22 m) apart. Today the stones survive but are utterly obscured by hummocky tussocks, and it is uncertain whether they can be claimed as chevaux-de-frise.
Anderson 1901, 144
RCAMS 1011a, 15, no. 35

Broch of Ness, Canisbay
National Grid reference ND 382666

Another of Tress Barry's. The isthmus is blocked by a ditch with a strong stone wall behind it; in the ditch there is a well and traces of what seem to be secondary structures. On the promontory seaward of the broch are various parallel ridges and depressions, with other running at right angles from them. It is very difficult to make anything of these features, which are concealed by long grass, but they may represent rectangular buildings.
Anderson 1901, 143
RCAMS 1911a, 13, no. 33

Sgarbach, Canisbay
National Grid reference ND 373658

On the coast near Aukingill is an L-shaped cliff-promontory. It curves around so that its far end lies parallel with the mainland, which is slightly higher; the defensive wall is situated well towards the landward end where there is no disadvantage of slope. It now appears as a broad mound across the isthmus (fig. 8), but when seen by Curle, doing the fieldwork for the RCAMS Inventory, it was not long excavated by Sir Francis Tress Barry, and the features were well-preserved and clear. Curle gives the wall-rampart a thickness of 12 feet 6 inches (3.81 m), a length of 62 feet (18.9 m) and a height of 5 feet (1.22 m). At the centre it is pierced by an entrance passage, now very dilapidated, described in 1911 as 3 feet 2 inches (0.97 m) wide at the outer end, 4 feet 9 inches (1.45 m) at the inner, with doorcheck and sill half-way through. There was a deep barhole in the wall beside the check. Behind the passage was an oval chamber in which were found a hearth and occupation debris, and an underfloor drain led out from this area through the entrance passage to the exterior of the fort. As it now appears, the masonry of the entrance passage consists of very thick, long slabs at the base, with smaller slabs higher up. Various mounds on either side of the rampart are probably excavation spoil. It is unfortunate that the site was left open after excavation, to which cause is attributable its present poor condition.
RCAMS 1911a, 18, no. 45
Ordnance Survey index ref. ND 36 SE 5

Broch of Nybster, Wick
National Grid reference ND 370631

The most remarkable feature of the site today is a fantastic fairy-castle monument ornamented with grotesque sculptures, erected by Sir Francis Tress Barry after his excavation, and now an historical monument in itself. The solid-based broch is built immediately seaward of a massive stone wall which sweeps across the cliff-promontory in a broad curve; it has an entrance passage with two sets of doorchecks.
Anderson 1901, 139
RCAMS 1911a, 159, no. 518
Hamilton 1968, 60

Gote o' Tram, Wick
National Grid reference ND 367480

The promontory, between long narrow geos, has a slight downslope to seaward. Across the narrowest point is a deep rock-cut ditch with a reserved causeway on the S side. On the inner lip of the ditch is a turf bank, rising 2.4 m above the ditch bottom and 0.9 m above the level ground behind. The approach to the promontory landward of the ditch runs through a slight hollow between turf banked up on either side, but this disturbance may be recent.

Bay of Girston, Wick
National Grid reference ND 364474

At the head of the Bay of Girston, and towards the S, a piece of land rises sharply to seaward but is cut off abruptly at the cliff edge; the cliff is over 45 m high and overhangs dangerously. To landward there is a steep slope 2.4 m high to a broad level terrace, in front of which is a V-sectioned ditch 1.8 m deep, running for some 35 m from edge to edge of the cliff. Although it may follow a fault-line, the ditch appears to be artificial. It is likely that the overhanging cliff is all that remains of what once was a promontory.

ORKNEY

Brough of Braebister, Hoy
National Grid reference HY 213052

A small headland 15 m high extends NW from the coast near the mouth of the Braebister burn. Across its landward end in a broad arc runs a mound 3.5 m high. This is described in the RCAMS Inventory as "modern, and consists apparently of the smaller stones which it was not worth carrying away from the structure" (i.e. from the broch which is assumed to have stood at the seaward end of the promontory). This is most unlikely; in the mound, particularly near its S end, portions of walling and occasional erect slabs are visible, and in front of it on the N side a low bank extends from the cliff edge and curves around to the NW to merge into the main mound. Landward of this bank there is a shallow ditch.

At the seaward end of the promontory there is nothing to suggest a broch. The promontory however is covered with settings of erect slabs, now mere stumps in the grass, which are set at right angles to one another, forming rectangular patterns. Just behind the main mound above the cliff on the S side, is a limpet-shell midden.
RCAMS 1946, ii, 109, no. 380

Castle of Burwick, South Ronaldsay
National Grid reference ND 435843

The Castle is a peninsular rock lying parallel to the shore at the S end of South Ronaldsay, accessible by a rock-bridge at the N end. Low in 1774 reported it as the site of a fortification, but it was too thickly grassed over for him to be able to say exactly what was there; the vegetation is just as bad today. The rock-bridge is defended by three dump banks with two intermediate ditches which now are about 0.9 m below the tops of the banks. At the summit of the steep slope on to the promontory there seems to have been an inner rampart (not shown on the RCAMS plan, fig. 20). The summit area immediately behind, is occupied by ill-defined structures, with stone structures extending down to the cliff-edge behind; these have been distorted by slip-faulting but can be seen to be built of erect slabs with dry walling above. They are quite considerable, and suggest houses rather than burial cists. Extending S along the promontory is a vague row of oblong foundations

probably relating to an early mediaeval monastic occupation. A rim sherd of coarse pottery, picked up during the RCAMS visit in 1929, is in Tankerness House, Kirkwall.
Low 1879, 28
RCAMS 1946, ii, 285, no. 817

Brough of Windwick, South Ronaldsay
National Grid reference ND 458873

The Brough is a narrow headland projecting from the precipitous cliffs, 45 m high, on the N side of Wind Wick (fig. 18). It lies near the boundary between hill pasture and infield. The isthmus is defended on the S side by four scooped-out, U-sectioned ditches with three intervening ramparts, and on the N, by two such ditches with one rampart between them. The central entrance path runs between the two sets of ditches. The ramparts are of turf, and retain a near-vertical profile, standing up to 2.5 m above the ditch bottoms. Immediately inward of the last ditches is a low bank going right across, and there is another bank 9 m further seaward. From the bottom of the inner ditch on the N side to the top of the bank is a height of nearly 5 m. The promontory is approached on the level and the ditches appear to be wholly artificial, being cut into the thick drift cap; but the inner N ditch at any rate, is cut through into the rock. The site is overgrown and no structures are visible within the fort.

Brough of Bigging, Yesnaby, Sandwick
National Grid reference HY 218158

A broad cliff-promontory which rises from a low isthmus to a height of 30 m at the seaward end, is separated from the land by a broad rift the bottom of which is only a metre or so above high-water mark. Immediately seaward of the rift is a broad bank, about 4.3 m wide and 0.5 m high, with traces of a stone revetment on the inner side. Some 30 m seaward, at the narrowest point of the promontory, is a second bank, rather larger than the first, with a well-marked entrance gap. In front of and around the entrance are numerous stone slabs set on edge, in a manner which cannot now be interpreted as any coherent structure (fig. 7). High up on the extremity of the promontory, near the modern navigation cairn, are structures represented only by widely scattered earthfast erect slabs of which only the stumps remain.
RCAMS 1946 ii, 267, no. 730

Broch of Borwick, Yesnaby, Sandwick
National Grid reference HY 224167

Before excavation in the 1880s the site, on a triangular cliff-headland, appeared as a large green mound; the excavations by Mr. W. G. T. Watt, of Skaill, involved the partial clearance of the broch tower and outbuildings. In front of the broch a broad depression cuts across the promontory, with, between it and the broch, a massively broad mound. This at one point can

be seen to have a stone facing, and an irregular hut seems to have been inserted into it.
Watt, 1882
RCAMS 1946, ii, 252, no. 679

Taing of Onstan, Stenness
National Grid reference HY 283117

The flat, low-lying promontory extending into the Loch of Stenness N of the well-known Onstan chambered tomb, is cut off by two banks each 0.6—0.9 m high, of loose material derived from shallow ditches inwards from them. Nothing else is visible on the 0.6-ha promontory, which is good pasture. A section across the banks was cut by the late Dr. F. T. Wainwright during the early 1960s. The excavation notes are lost, but were seen by the compiler of the Ordnance Survey index entry who has retailed Wainwright's conclusion that the promontory had been the site of a "nesnám". The drawn section is reproduced on the index card, and it shows merely simple dump banks with traces of stone revetments.
RCAMS 1946, ii, 273, no. 873
Ordnance Survey index ref. HY 21 SE 22

Nether Bigging, Stenness
National Grid reference HY 301119

This is in a situation similar to that of Onstan, above. It is another low promontory on the same shore of the loch, about 1.5 km E. Excavations in 1924-5 revealed a wall with external ditch across the isthmus, and stone structures at the loch end of the promontory. Clouston identified these as remains of a mediaeval castle, but his plan shows an indeterminate confusion of structures and no datable finds were made during the dig. But according to RCAMS a sherd of so-called "broch" pottery was picked up on the site. The site is now subject to constant flooding.
Clouston 1936
RCAMS 1946, ii, 298, no. 874
Ordnance Survey index ref. HY 31 SW 36

Castle of Sand Geo, Copinsay
National Grid reference HY 612017

On the N shore of the small island of Copinsay, which now is inhabited only by the lighthouse-keepers, there is a broad sandy geo enclosed on the W side by a curved promontory (fig. 25). From the beach, on which a small boat can land, is an easy slope up to the neck of the promontory, which itself rises to a height of rather over 6 m. About half-way up the approach slope is a wall, up to 0.9 m high, its stones eroded and moss-covered and having an ancient appearance. The wall is built against the slope and its top forms a level terrace. At the E end, there is a confusion of tumble in which it is not clear whether the wall continues to the cliff, or curves inwards to flank

the entrance. Above the wall, the crest of the slope is crowned by a broad rampart which now stands 0.6 m above the level of the ground inside. The cliff-section reveals that the rampart has a core of carefully-laid stones with a revetment on either face. Immediately behind the rampart is a semicircular depression against the cliff, apparently a truncated hut-circle. N of here is a recent-looking hole, suggested by the Ordnance Survey as the find-spot of a stone axe now in Tankerness House museum, Kirkwall. The hole was stated by Mr. J. R. Foubister, farmer, of Skaill, Deerness, to be the temporary grave of a body, since exhumed, which was washed up in Sand Geo during the last war. At the end of the promontory there are many earthfast erect slabs and a short length of wall cutting off the extreme tip.
Mooney 1926
Ordnance Survey index ref. HY 50 SW 5

Riggan of Kami, Deerness
National Grid reference HY 593074

In the centre of a small cliffbound bay is a detached stack, the Moustag, towards which there runs a long, narrow promontory called Riggan of Kami. Closing the approach to the promontory is a considerable structure, which however is obscured by lush vegetation. It appears as a very broad mound, some 1.5 m high, extending in a wide arc across the promontory. By kicking through the vegetation it is possible to locate disconnected lengths of walling, including what seems to be an end wall-face delimiting the N extremity of the mound. Some of the portions of wall seem to belong to small oval chambers within the mound. RCAMS reports that a ruined stair once was visible; but from the shape of the mound it is clear that this is not a broch. Immediately seaward of the mound are some possible huts and in the summit of the promontory, which rapidly narrows to a knife-edge, there are occasional earthfast erect slabs. It is not clear whether the promontory connected with the stack at the time of occupation; the stack summit is occupied by a large circular structure, and while this could be connected with the fort, it is at least equally possible that it is monastic.
RCAMS 1946, ii, 243, no. 628.

Brough of Deerness
National Grid reference HY 596087

This is a well-known eremitic monastic settlement consisting of an extensive complex of longhouses surrounding a small oratory; these structures as we now see them probably represent a monastery, most likely Benedictine, of the twelfth or thirteenth century. There is however the possibility of earlier Christian occupation and the site, on a cliff-promontory, may in origin have been a prehistoric fort of which the massive "vallum monasterii", which runs along the land-facing edge of the headland, may be a relic. The idea of pre-monastic occupation as a "rock-fort" was suggested by George Low in 1774.
Low 1879, 55
RCAMS 1946, ii, 240, no. 621

Broch of Midhowe, Rousay
National Grid reference HY 370308

Midhowe, the central one of a set of three close-spaced brochs, is sited on a small promontory between narrow geos. The broch is built close behind a massive stone forework, which at ist base is 4.3 m to 5.8 m thick, the wallfaces being battered, and at the S end increases in width to 9 m where is the entrance passage. It seems that no attempt has been made to ascertain whether this structure is solid or hollow.
Callander and Grant 1934
RCAMS 1946, ii, 193, no. 553
Hamilton 1968, 60

(unnamed fort) Stronsay
National Grid reference HY 690235

This narrow promontory slopes gently down from the land towards the sea. Across it is a single stone-revetted rampart behind which are outlines of small irregular huts and erect slabs haphazardly placed. It seems that at some time this site has been claimed as that of a chapel, but as the Ordnance Survey index card has been missing for some time the source of this suggestion has not been traced.
Ordnance Survey index ref. HY 62 SE 18

SHETLAND

The Landberg, Fair Isle
National Grid reference HZ 223723

The Landberg is a narrow promontory with sheer cliffs rising about 25m from South Haven, which with the neighbouring North Haven provides just about the best harbourage on the island. The promontory slopes gradually up from the land, and is cut across by a natural rift beyond which is a very steep slope up to the level plateau which forms the defended area. Landward of the rift, the approach is guarded by a series of banks made of loose stony material derived from shallow intermediate ditches. E of the entrance path there are three of these banks with two ditches, there being no ditch in front of the outermost rampart. At the W end of the inner one, there are two large boulders set against the path. All three banks are of uniform height, standing about 1.2 m at their highest above the ditch bottoms. W of the entrance path there is a single horseshoe-plan bank extending out from the cliff edge to flank the path (fig. 14).

The rift, already a considerable obstacle, has been deepened with a vertical-sided artificial cutting, which has at least 0.3 m of silt in the bottom. There is a reserved causeway in line with the entrance path, which then climbs straight up the steep slope to the summit, where the entrance through the main rampart is on the same alignment. This rampart is broader and stone-revetted, and between it and the crest of the slope is a distinct berm. The entrance passage is stone-lined, and behind it is a substantial rectangular foundation, 6.7 m x 4.3 m internally with walls 1.2 m thick. This probably represents

a secondary occupation. Beyond the building, occupying most of the remainder of the defended area, is a string of shallow depressions possibly representing huts, and on the E side is an extensive midden deposit. Some sherds of coarse pottery found in this area are in the National Museum of Antiquities, Edinburgh.
RCAMS 1946, iii, 46, no. 1194

Ness of Burgi, Scatness, Dunrossness
National Grid reference HU 388084

Scatness is a long, low-lying and rocky promontory forming the W side of the West Voe of Sumburgh. The cliffs, varying from one metre to some fifteen metres in height, are jagged and reef-beset. Ness of Burgi is a subsidiary promontory extending E from the main one near its S end; some 150 m before the fort is reached, the main promontory is barred by a low stone-revetted bank. The fort itself was excavated in the 1930s and the blockhouse restored in 1971 by the Department of the Environment; the restoration was in some respects unfortunate and the new masonry cannot now be distinguished from the old. Before the restoration the blockhouse was over 22.5 m long, its SW end being destroyed by sea erosion. On the NE side its end wall-face is well back from the cliff edge. There is a lintelled entrance passage at the centre, and three cells are preserved in the thickness of the structure. The blockhouse stands at the crest of a short sharp slope at the foot of which are two rock-cut ditches with a heavy, revetted rampart between them, the entrance path passing through these obstacles by a gap in line with the passage in the blockhouse. Behind the blockhouse no deposits survived on the promontory, which had been wave-scoured to the bare rock. (Fig. 4).
Mowbray 1936
RCAMS 1946, iii, 34, no. 1154
Hamilton 1968, 58-9

North Fort, Scatness, Dunrossness
National Grid reference HU 389088

This site lies on the E side of Scatness some 400 m N of Ness of Burgi. The fort is sited on a blunt headland which is closed off by a curving bank, 1.5 m high and 3 m broad at base, made of loose material derived from a broad shallow internal quarry-scoop (fig. 12). The main feature is a broad structure crowning a low rise on the extremity of the headland; it is cut by the cliff on the E side but does not extend all the way to the cliff edge on the W. The section on the E cliff-edge coincides with an end wall-face of good masonry with a foundation course of orthostats. Otherwise the structure appears only as a mound, but the front of it can be seen to have a stone facing. The low-lying area behind it has been subject to wave-scour.

Sumburgh Head, Dunrossness
National Grid reference HU 408080

George Low saw the site in 1774 and states that it had been fortified. 'Here the neck of land is cut off by a ditch and strong wall, which must in

old times have formed a considerable fortification. It encloses a plain and hill (the Head); at the entrance, still observable the foundation of a large house, which probably served as a guardroom, along the wall, and at a distance, the marks of numerous small buildings, exactly like those described in Unst". By the buildings in Unst he means a set of oblong foundations on the high headland of Blue Mull, a site which falls into the pattern of early monastic settlements typified by such sites as Birrier of West Sandwick and Kame of Isbister (Lamb 1973). It does seem however that at Sumburgh Low saw something which represented a promontory-fort occupation. The oblong buildings must have been on the site of the lighthouse and its associated buildings, but some defences survived on the approach to the headland until 1968 when a new road was made. Shortly before this, they were described by the Ordnance Survey as "traces of two stony ramparts, with external ditches, on narrowest part of neck".
Low 1879, 185
RCAMS 1946, iii, 45, no. 1189
Ordnance Survey index ref. HU 40 NW 1

Broch of Burraland, Dunrossness
National Grid reference HU 477233

The broch, really a galleried dun, is built on the summit of a promontory which is approached over a very narrow isthmus. Across this is a modern sheepfold, to either side of which is the remains of a defensive barrier. The outer rampart is reduced to a height of 0.5 m, with a revetment of orthostats, while that immediately inwards from the sheepfold, and built on a sharp rise in the ground, is a stone wall, the end-face of which is visible above the cliff on the W side.
RCAMS 1946, iii, 24, no. 1143

Broch of Aithsetter, Dunrossness
National Grid reference HU 477304

The broch, sited on a cliff-promontory, is reduced to a green mound, and barring the isthmus approach are vestiges of defensive banks. These are clearly visible only on the S side, where there are two much-spread banks standing about 1.2 m above the bottom of the intervening V-sectioned ditch.
RCAMS 1946, iii, 23, no. 1141

Broch of Burland, Lerwick
National Grid reference HU 445360

The broch on a precipitous 30 m headland has three ramparts, each fronted by a ditch, on the isthmus before it. The entrance path is centrally placed and runs in a straight line through all three banks. The outer bank is stone-revetted and stands 1.8 m above the bottom of the flat-bottomed ditch outwards from its. The middle one is a dump and is rather slighter, while the inner rampart is a more substantial dump bank to the E of the path,

but on the W side is a well-built block of masonry which has an end-face above the cliff. (Fig. 20).
RCAMS 1946, iii, 70, no. 1247

Burrier Head, Waas
National Grid reference HU 169514

Burrier Head is a long level promontory with sheer cliffs. The isthmus is narrow and immediately beyond it is a wall; this may not be ancient, but it incorporates two enormous boulders, and the ground immediately behind is hummocky, with projecting erect slabs. In the cliff-section on the S side, stone structures and occupation debris are visible. Well seaward of this complex, there is a single erect slab, and further still, the very vestigial remains of a squarish building. The turf on the site is thick, and other structures may be concealed.

Brough Ness of Garth, Sandness
National Grid reference HU 216582

The promontory projects from a rugged coast backed by poor quality pasture. It is separated from the mainland by a boulder-beach across which exceptionally high seas run. The defences are set against the land-facing slope up to the headland (fig. 16). This slope has been terraced, with two terraces supported by massive retaining walls. At the summit of the slope, and running the full length of the landward side of the promontory, is a broad stone wall-foundation. All the walls are rather crudely built of rounded beach-boulders, those of the basal courses being larger and treated as orthostats. The position of the entrance is not clear; it may have been to the E of the terrace-walls.

Behind the defences on the W side is a group of buildings. Immediately within the uppermost wall are three circular houses each about 3 m diameter, and an oblong one, just over 6 m long internally. Another oblong one has almost gone over the cliff, the length of its surviving complete side being 2.4 m between rounded corners. All these buildings are quite substantially constructed of good stone. The promontory divides into two spurs at the seaward end; across the W spur is a low turf bank and a vestigial structure, some 3 m square, also of turf.
RCAMS 1946, iii, 152, no. 1663 (negative report)
Ordnance Survey index ref. HU 25 NW 2

Hog Island Sound, Neap, Nesting
National Grid reference HU 508582

The broad headland extending E from the farmlands of Neap is continued eastwards as Hog Island, from which it is separated by a gulf 13 m wide. The cliffs are about 12 m high on the mainland side and 15 m on the island side. The island is cliffbound and can be visited by boat only during exceptionally calm weather. The fortifications, which were discovered in 1968 by Mr.

W. B. Johnston of the Ordnance Survey, lie partly on the mainland and partly on the island (fig. 15).

On the mainland the defences are three unrevetted dump banks, each up to 3 m broad and 0.5 to 1 m high, the outermost bank being on average slightly larger than the other two, although the innermost one has been cut in half longitudinally by erosion at the cliff edge. The banks, standing about 4.5 m apart, are built of material derived from shallow intervening scoops which are flat-bottomed and seem to represent the removal only of the few inches of soil and the topmost, friable layer of bedrock. At the mid point the banks are pierced by an entrance path running in a straight line through all three. There are large boulders set in the middle rampart beside the entrance, and the path passes between two even larger ones in the inner bank, where now it ends abruptly at the cliff edge.

The island is inaccessible, but along the land-facing edge, and curving around the N side, is visible another bank, this one revetted with large stones. The entrance gap seems to have been directly opposite the path. Nothing else is visible on the island.
Ordnance Survey index ref. HU 55 NW 2

Brough of Stoal, Aywick, Yell
National Grid reference HU 546873

The site is a narrow promontory with cliffs 45 m high between deep geos. The fragmentary remains noted by RCAMS on its extremity do not suggest a broch, but a complex of structures built partly of slabs and partly of masonry. The defences are simple and impressive, comprising three dump ramparts separated by ditches which now appear flat-bottomed but which contain silt (fig.17). The banks stand nowhere less them 2.1 m high, the middle one rising to over 3.7 m above its ditch. There is no trace of an entrance, which must have been on one of the sides lost through erosion. A fourth rampart on the E side may have been associated with it, but of this outermost rampart only a small fragment is left. The banks are of loose material and damage by rabbits is serious.
RCAMS 1946, iii, 161, no. 1717.

Burgi Geos, West Neaps, Yell
National Grid reference HP 477034

This fort, which must be just about the most remotely-sited fort in Shetland, occupies a long sinuous promontory between deep and precipitous geos, with cliffs 60 m high. The rock, a gneiss heavily laden with muscovite and veined with quartzite, is extremely hard and brittle and when eroded gives a jagged outline. The path runs along the narrow isthmus, where the outer defences are placed, then descends to cross a lower and narrower saddle before climbing to the main structure, which is a blockhouse (fig. 10).

The outer defences form an avenue on either side of the path. On the N there is a continuous line of stones presenting an even face to the path, on the

S is a bank set with a coarse chevaux-de-frise of jagged stones; E of this bank, also beside the path, is a curious free-standing trapezoidal-plan mound. The blockhouse contains no gateway and is 4.25 m wide by 6.7 m long; it is not certain whether it is solid or hollow but probably hollow. From its NE corner a slight ringwall, only a few courses high, runs flush with the front face of the blockhouse; this curves around, following the edge of the cliff and returns to join the SW corner of the blockhouse where it is flush with the S end-face; the abutments are straight joints, not bonded. Within the narrow enclosure thus formed behind the blockhouse, a rich growth of grass suggests occupation.

To seaward are indications of round huts. The most marked of these is bisected by the cliff edge and the erosion section shows occupation debris overlain by 0.23 m of sterile peat. Some sherds of coarse pottery from this section are in the Shetland Museum, Lerwick.

The badly faulted condition of the precipice on the very brink of which the blockhouse now stands, is a matter of very serious concern; the site is an important one and deserves a rescue excavation while the chance still remains.

Some readers may contemplate a visit to Burgi Geos and in the interests of safety, it is as well here to include a word about access to the site. The place has appeared in two different "archaeological guides", one Scottish one and the other concerned only with Orkney and Shetland, and in both books directions are given that the site is to be approached across moorland NW from Dalsetter. It must be assumed that the authors had never been to Yell, for this course would lead the visitor into serious difficulties amid the notorious Cuilag Mires. The writer has tried several routes and the best is as follows: From Bridge of Dalsetter follow the burn of the Gossa Water upstream, and skirt the N shore of the Gossa Water loch, then strike due W to the coast which is to be followed N to the fort. Needless to say, a map and compass should be carried and normal hillwalking precautions taken. The coastline is precipitous and despite a suggestion in one of the guidebooks, there is no landing by boat.

RCAMS 1946, iii, 163, no. 1724
Harbison 1971

Brough of Borgastoon, Fetlar
National Grid reference HU 616873

A long narrow promontory with cliffs 45 m high is defended on the land side of its narrow isthmus (which is pierced by a natural arch) by two earth banks each fronted by a ditch. They do not extend completely across the approach but on the W side their ends are joined by a cross-bank which flanks the approach path (fig. 19). The banks stand about 1.2 m—1.5 m above the ditch bottoms. On the promontory there are hummocks and earthfast erect slabs, including a possible parapet along the E side, but nothing to suggest a broch.

Ordnance Survey index ref. Hu 68 NW 2

Aithbank, Fetlar
National Grid reference HU 642897

The small promontory S of Aithbank farmstead, between the Wick of Aith and Aiths Lee, has been enclosed by three banks of loose material. They are each 1.5 m high on the E side and peter out westwards. They are hard to explain as agricultural and probably constitute the remains of a small fort which has been greatly reduced by old cultivation.

Taing of Brough, Flubersgerdie, Unst
National Grid reference HP 571125

The promontory (fig. 13) is high and narrow between the precipitous Geos of Brough. The path approaches across a narrow saddle. About two-thirds of the way up the steep slope to the summit there are remains of a stone wall, now at most four courses high, running across. Behind it on the summit is a very hummocky area with projecting stones. Towards the seaward end of the promontory are two oblong footings, one 4.6 m x 7.6 m of turf and stone, the other 3m x 8.5 m of turf only. At the SW end of the first oblong is another, roughly square, depression.

The large headland of which the Taing is an extension, the Flubersgerdie, is isolated by a broad marshy depression, on the seaward edge of which is a ruined wall built of quite exceptionally massive boulders.
RCAMS 1946, iii, 143, no. 1593
Ordnance Survey index ref. HP 51 SE 1

Krun o' de Øra, Unst
National Grid reference HP 634179

North of Saxa Vord, a long narrow promontory extends seawards for 0.7 km, culminating in spectacular crags over 140 m high. There have been reports of a "brough" at the landward end of the promontory, but the area has suffered from landslides and what remains is rather indeterminate.

Jakobsen wrote that "north of the hill Saksavord the land narrows, and juts out like a tongue ending in a promontory, "de Nup". Between Saksavord and "de Nup" there is a hill called "de Øra", steep on the E side, but sloping gently towards the W. The top of the hill is round and flat, and is called "de Krun o' de Øra", where the ruins of a Pictish tower are found. On the western side of the hill a burial chamber ("Picts' House") was found some time ago. At the foot of the western side of the hill there are traces of three old stone-fences, running in a semicircle, one inside the other; and one of these fences, which is a little better preserved than the two others, can be traced all the way to the coast on the south-east side of "de Øra". In several places in Shetland traces of such concentric fences, surrounding a Pictish tower, can be seen. Just underneath the place where the fence ends there is a cave called "de heljer o' Fivlagord" which is feared by the common people as a trolls' cave. Fivlagord from an old *fiflagardr: troll-fence (ON fifl, troll) is thus the old name of the fence ..."

RCAMS quotes a report from a Dr. Hunt, who described "a sort of natural broch, protected by a wall running down to the sea on the land side". No such wall is visible today and the Ordnance Survey reports no ancient structures of any kind.

The promontory takes the form of a series of level platforms connected by lower and narrower saddles. The first platform from the land, that recorded by Jakobsen as "de Krun o' de Øra", does show indeterminate signs of occupation. There is a stout bank across the land-facing end, and traces of a parapet along the N side, with some possible huts within the enclosure. The rest of the promontory is badly broken-up by slip faulting, but the association with "da trows" is a good indication of some kind of ancient occupation.
Jakobsen 1936, 170
RCAMS 1946, iii, 139, no. 1572
Ordnance Survey index ref. HP 61 NW 4

APPENDIX 2

Nesnám

The idea that Viking sea-raiders established promontory forts from which to raid along the coast or inland, has enjoyed a surprisingly long currency. Very little is known about the actual process by which the Norse settlement of Orkney and Shetland took place, and there is no archaeological evidence that any promontory fort belongs to this early Viking period. Neither is there any real historical evidence for promontory-fort building; the idea originates in an interpretation of the word nesnám, "ness-taking" which occurs in the sagas.

J. Storer Clouston, in his "History of Orkney" (1932, 19) wrote: "One of the most characteristic features of the professional Viking's methods was what is termed in the sagas "nes-nám", litterally "ness-taking". They seized upon a ness with a narrow neck that could be readily defended on the landward side, converting it into a pirates' lair, and made it their headquarters for operations, either against their neighbours or further afield". In the early 1960s, the late Dr. F. T. Wainwright investigated by low-lying fortified promontory at Onstan (fig. 20) in the Loch of Stenness. The excavation notes are lost, but were used as the basis for the Ordnance Survey card index entry, which has preserved both the excavation details and Wainwright's interpretation of Taing of Onstan as the site of a nesnám. The section which Wainwright cut across the defences, showed a stone revetment to the bank, suggesting that this is something more than a temporary earthwork thrown up in a hurry; no dating material emerged, but the resemblance to the coastal multivallate forts makes an Early Iron Age date much more likely. The Taing of Onstan is not well placed as an encampment for seaborne raiders, from which they might presumably escape if things got too hot; for the only entrance to the Loch of Stenness is the narrow strait at Brig' o' Waith, and it is doubtful that even at high tide a seagoing vessel could make the passage. Even if a Viking ship did manage to get into the Loch of Stenness, she would be seriously at risk of being trapped there.

The precise meaning of nesnám is uncertain—the three references given by Cleasby and Vigfusson's Icelandic distionary do not suggest that it has a precise meaning:

Hafđi Þórólfr þá þrjú skip, er hann sigldi austan um Foldina; sigldu þá þjóđleiđ til Liđandisnes; fóru þá sem skyndiligast, en námu nesnám, þar sem þeir kómu vid, ok hjuggu strandhǫgg. (Egils Saga 19).

Then Thorolf had three ships as he sailed from the east round Foldina; they sailed by the main seaway to Lithandisness; they came there with great speed, and wherever they landed they committed nesnám and strandhogg.

En í þann tíma var mjǫk herskátt, því at Norðmenn ok Danir herjuðu mjǫk i vestrvíking ok kómu optliga við eyjarnar, er þeir fóru vestr eða vestan, ok námu þar nesnám. (Orkneyinga Saga 19).

At that time there was a lot of warfare, because the Norwegians and Danes were doing much harrying as they went about their west-viking, and often came among the islands as they were sailing west or east, and committed nesnám there.

En bæði á haust ok um vetr ok um vár fóru víkingar um eyjar, námu nesnám ok hjoggu strandhǫgg. (Heimskringla, Harald Fairhair 27).

And both in autumn and in winter and in spring the vikings sailed around the isles, committing nesnám and strandhogg.

In two of the three instances, nesnám appears in conjunction with strandhogg in what looks like a saga-writers' cliché—nema nesnám ok hoggva strandhogg, literally to "take ness-taking and hew strand-hewing". It is a poetic phrase for general plundering, possibly, as Cleasby and Vigfussion suggest, undertaken on outlying headlands where the inhabitants had less chance of help from neighbours. Certainly, there is no suggestion that it involved building fortifications; in any event, organised heavy shovel-work after the manner of an encamping Roman legion, seems hardly in character with the saga picture of a husky crew of Vikings. Viking-Age nesnám therefore does not provide a context for promontory-fort construction in the Northern Isles.

APPENDIX 3

THE CAITHNESS GROUP OF EARLY PROMONTORY-SITED CASTLES

On the coasts of Caithness and the neighbouring part of Sutherland there is a concentration of mediaeval castles of a most romantic type, built on precipitous cliff-promontories. Their common characteristic is that each has a great tower built at the landward end of a promontory guarding the isthmus approach, and protecting the ranges of domestic buildings on the promontory behind it. It is possible that three of these structures, Borve Castle in Sutherland and the Castles of Brough and Old Wick in Caithness, are earlier than is generally supposed, while a fourth, Bucholie Castle, may overlie the site of an early castle.

The Castle of Old Wick or "Old Man of Wick" (National Grid reference ND 370489; fig. 26, plates 23-4) was described by MacGibbon and Ross (1889, 134-6) as "very simple and rude, and probably the oldest of all the existing castles of Caithness". Its main feature is a plain square tower built on the landward end of a 30 m-high, narrow promontory between two precipitous geos. The tower is built on the brink of a steep-sided, flat-bottomed ditch some 8.5 m wide and 3 m deep, cut into the rock right across the promontory. Landward of this ditch there is disturbance, but it is not clear how much is ancient and how much is due to recent dumping of rubbish. The approach path crosses the ditch on a reserved saddle and then passes beside the great tower, where there is now no indication of whatever form of gateway has existed. Behind the tower is a long range of buildings extending down each side of the promontory, leaving a broad central pathway which is finally terminated, well short of the extremity of the promontory, by a low wall. The only purpose of this wall will presumably have been to keep the castle children from straying near the cliff edge. The buildings are entirely grassed over and it is not clear to what extent the rather schematised-looking plan by A. Miller, incorporated in MacGibbon and Ross's account, is an accurate representation of them; the writer's plan shows the site as it appeared in 1971.

Borve Castle, on the deserted N coast of Sutherland near Farr (pl. 25; RCAMS 1911b, 89, no. 264; National Grid reference NC 725642) stands on a peninsula which is joined to the mainland by a considerably lower saddle. At the beginning of the slope up to the promontory is a bank across the approach; this bank is almost entirely a natural outcrop although it may have been artificially scarped and to some extent built up. At the head of the slope is the remnant of a small plain square tower occupying most of the width of the isthmus, leaving space for the path which passes by on its E side. The keep is built of dressed blocks each about 0.5 m square, bonded with lime mortar, and behind and adjoining the tower is a short range of buildings in the same style of masonry. The seaward end of the peninsula slopes steeply down to

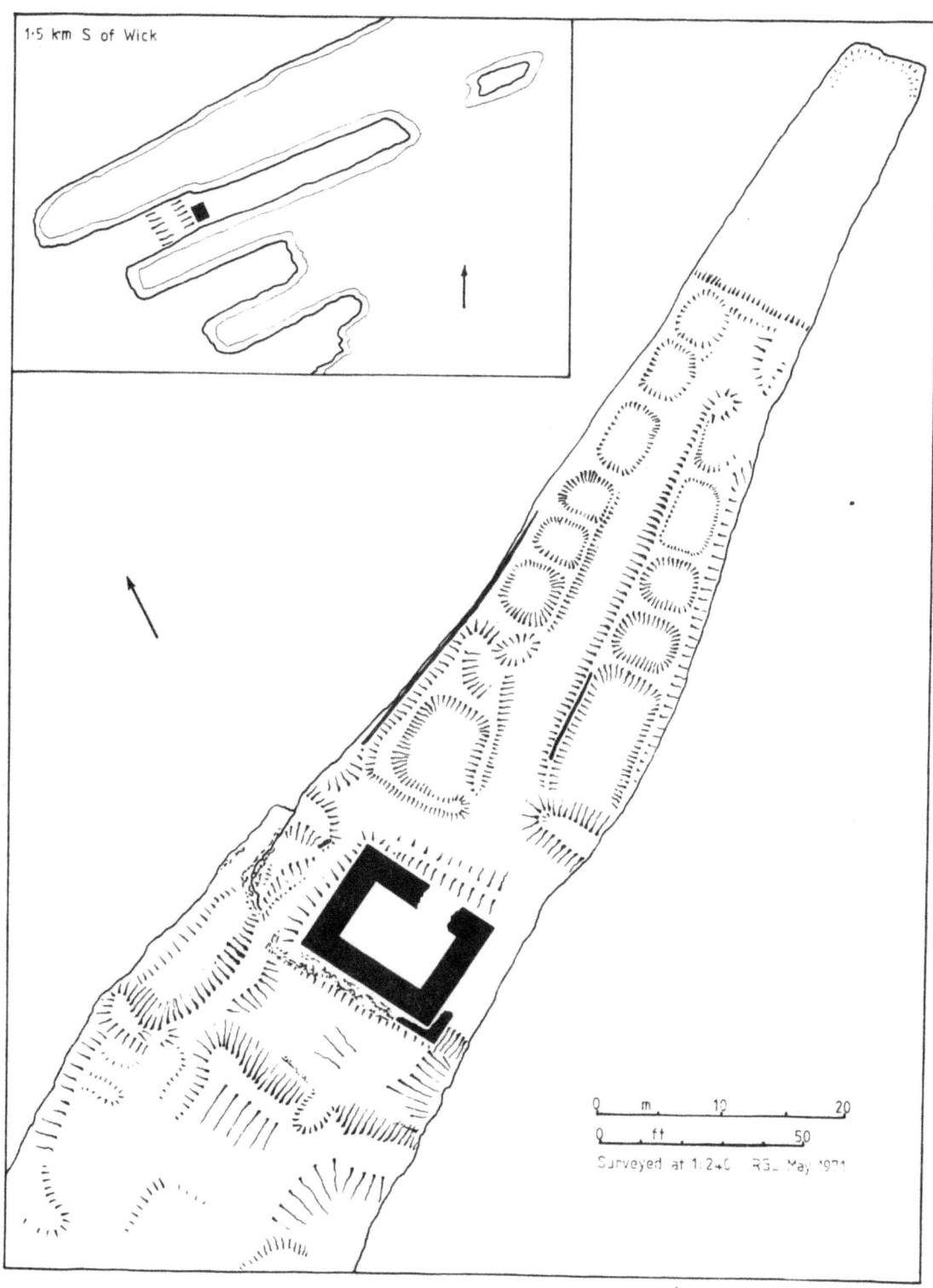

Fig. 26. Castle of Old Wick, Caithness.

shelving rocks and to preclude any possibility of attack from the sea, a ditch has been dug across, with a slight bank to either side of it; the height of the inner bank above the ditch bottom is about 1.8 m.

The Castle of Brough, immediately E of Dunnet Head (pl. 26; RCAMS 1911a, 27, no. 82; National Grid reference ND 228740), is less well-preserved, probably because its close proximity to the crofting township of Brough has led to the robbing of all cut stones. The site is a long narrow promontory very like Old Wick but not so high, across the neck of which is a broad natural depression which has been further excavated to form a considerable flat-bottomed ditch. At the head of the slope on to the promontory, in the position corresponding to that of the keep at Old Wick and Borve, is a large mound of debris, and seawards from here two ranges of buildings, in size and arrangement exactly like those at Old Wick, extend along the sides of the promontory leaving a central pathway. At the end, where the surface slopes down to rocks above the sea, the slope has been steeply scarped, a bank being made at the summit of the scarp and a ditch excavated at its foot, very much as at Borve.

The arrangement of a great tower guarding the approach to a cliff-promontory, with ranges of buildings extending along the clifftops behind it—an arrangement largely dictated by the limitations of the sites—is found also in the much better-preserved Caithness castles of Bucholie (RCAMS 1911a, 11, no. 32; National Grid reference ND 382658) and the double castle of Girnigoe and Sinclair (RCAMS 1911a, 139, no. 479; National Grid reference ND 379549). Here however the keeps are typically Scottish tower-houses of the fifteenth or sixteenth centuries, each entirely closing the isthmus approach and serving as a gatehouse with a wide entrance-passage, equipped with the usual paraphernalia of drawbridges and portcullises and so on, running through the ground floor. The distinctive feature of Borve and Old Wick, and apparently of Brough, is that the keep, a plain square tower, stood beside the approach, acting as a focus of defence and protecting the buildings behind it, but not actually being a gatehouse. It is possible that here this notion is Scandinavian not Scottish, this group of castles therefore being earlier than has generally been thought.

MacGibbon and Ross put Old Wick into their "second period" of Scottish castle-building, the fourteenth century. There is not much to go on; the keep lacks readily datable features and its building is not documented. We know only that the first recorded owner of the property died c. 1350. The castles of Borve and Brough are entirely undocumented and excavation would be necessary to produce any dating evidence at all. Simple square towers used in a very similar way are however found in Scandinavia much earlier than the fourteenth century. The best-studied example is Sverresborg in Trondheim which was thoroughly excavated immediately before the last war (Fischer 1951, 68-85 and 292-314). It is built on a sheer-sided plateau, and consists of a range of buildings (the outer wall of this being the curtain wall) with a square tower occupying the central position in the range. The foundations of Sverresborg were laid in 1182-3. At Lilleborg in the forest of Almindingen in Bornholm (fig. 27) a craggy plateau is encircled by a ringwall against the inner side of which are domestic buildings, with the simple square tower projecting from the line of the ringwall close by the gate. Lilleborg, a royal castle, was destroyed and abandoned in 1259.

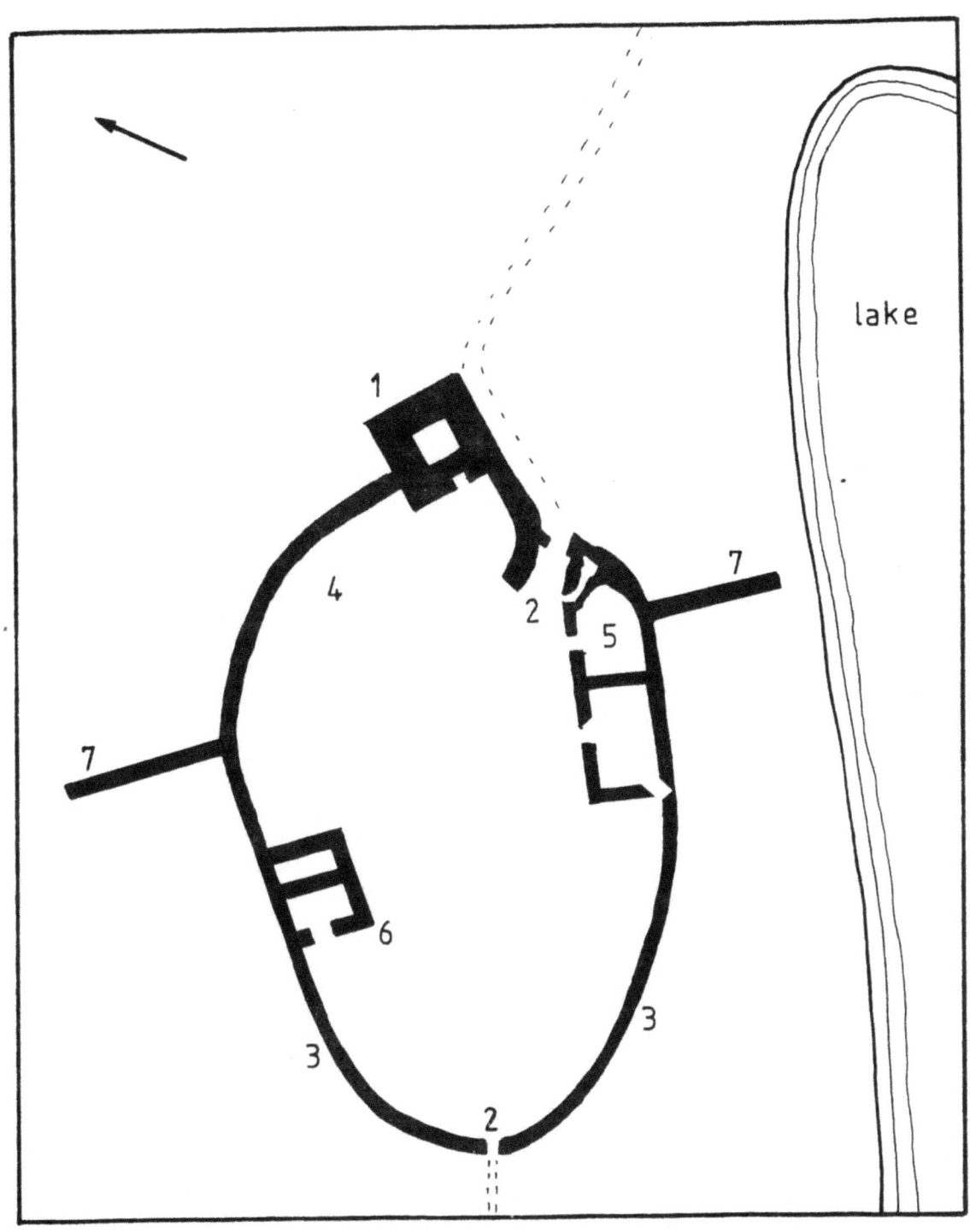

Fig. 27. Lilleborg, Almindingen, Bornholm, sketch-plan based on Danish National Museum display on the site. 1, great tower. 2, gateways. 3, ring-wall. 4, remains of older ring-wall. 5, main buildings. 6, other buildings. 7, flanking walls.

There are some small plain keeps in Orkney which possibly date from the late twelfth century onwards. The best-known of these is Cubbie Roo's castle in Wyre, the stronghold of the great chieftain Kolbein Hruga in the middle of the twelfth century, which consists of one of these towers, surrounded by buildings, nestling within a small enclosure on a hilltop (RCAMS 1946, ii, 235-9, no. 619). This structure does have direct saga documentation, and there are two other known towers in Orkney which resemble it. One of these is Castle Howe in Holm, where the remains of a strong tower stand on the summit of a prominent mound formed by some prehistoric structure, possibly a broch. The tower was excavated in 1929-31 and identified by Clouston (1931, 33-5) as a Norse castle, an identification accepted by Taylor (1938, 384), but the Royal Commission (RCAMS 1946, ii, 103-4, no. 361) remains uncommitted, referring to the structure as of uncertain age and avoiding any use of the word "castle". This is over-cautious, as the form of the square tower is even today obvious enough and the name, applied to a site such as this, can only be taken literally—kastala-haugr, castle-howe, kastali being the standard term in saga Icelandic for a mediaeval castle. In all probability it belonged to the important earldom seat of Papuli, which is mentioned several times in the Orkneyinga Saga and most likely stood at the head of the same bay, Howes Wick. The other Orkney tower is a rather enigmatic structure called The Wirk—from virki, a stronghold—near the ruined church at Westside in Rousay (RCAMS 1946, ii, 191-2, no. 550). This also was studied by Clouston (1931, 27-33) and evidently adjoined some larger building which was imperfectly examined and now is covered up. It is obviously a defensive structure and possibly was associated with a Norse establishment of some status at nearby Westness, but the suggestion that it served as a bell-tower to the church (Dietrichson and Meyer 1906, 108-9) deserves more serious consideration than it has received. Re-excavation would be necessary to solve the problem.

The Royal Commission draws attention to the difference in quality between the masonry of the tower of Cubbie Roo's Castle and that of the enclosure wall, and proposes that the enclosure is the original twelfth-century castle and the keep substantially later. The Commission admits the possibility of such towers being built in Orkney in Kolbein Hruga's time but, after a very scholarly discussion involving the Caithness keeps and some Continental parallels, feels it is unsafe to place this tower so early. Attention is drawn to the lack of obviously Romanesque features, but the tower is so plain that it has no features datable to any period. In a community which at this time was building in Kirkwall one of the finest Romanesque churches in Europe, we need not be surprised to find one of its most powerful magnates building a tower-keep. The saga account of the building (Orkneyinga Saga chapter 84) tells of Kolbein's erecting a good stone castle and a secure stronghold: "Hann lét bar gera steinkastala gódan; var bat oruggt vígi". In 1231 this castle was, according to Hakonar Saga (chapter 141 in Flatey version) involved in a siege; the garrison laid in provisions, including cattle, within the outer works (the outer castle, útkastali): "...í kastalann, er Kolbeinn hruga hafdi gera látit. Peir drógu at sér fǫng ok fjǫlda nauta ok vardveittu í útkastalanum". This does suggest that Kolbein's "stone-castle" had some "útkastali" distinct from the "kastali" proper; in other words, the tower and enclosure wall both date from the twelfth century.

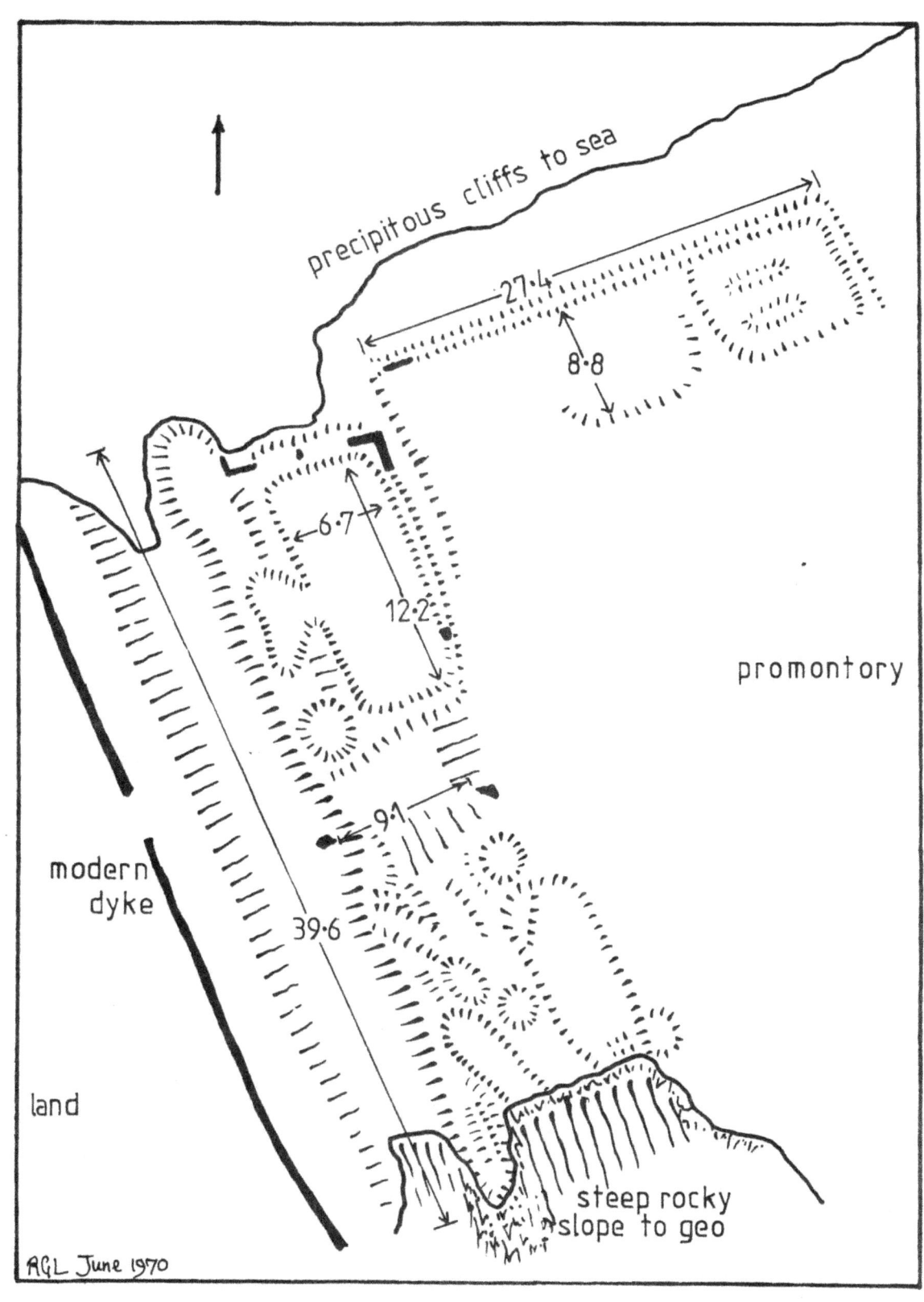

Fig. 28. Lambhoga Head, Dunrossness, Shetland, sketch-plan with measurements. (The plan was originally made using Imperial measurements which here have been converted to metric to the nearest 0.1 m.)

There is no mention in the sagas of any of the Caithness promontory castles, except for the incident of c. 1143 when the adventurer Sweyn Asleifsson, who was pillaging in Caithness, stood siege in the fortress of "Lambaborg" (Orkneyinga Saga, chs. 82-3). The place is not described as a "kastali" but as a "vígi" or a "borg", and it was a sea-girt cliff-promontory with a strong stone wall blocking the approach. Lambaborg ("the fortress of Lambi", a personal name) has generally been identified with Bucholie Castle by everyone except Taylor (1938, 390) who prefers the Broch of Ness, on the other side of Freswick bay. If Taylor is right, this implies the re-use of the Iron Age fortifications, the "stone wall" (steinveggr) presumably being the forework which, just as at Nybster, stands in front of the broch. If Bucholie is the correct identification, there is the suggestion that a twelfth-century castle had preceded the existing one. The circumstances related in the saga are not such as to enable the matter to be settled; the argument for Bucholie has been most clearly stated by Mowat (1940). It is however of interest that the older name of Bucholie Castle was Freswick Castle, suggesting a link with what evidently was a high-status establishment at Freswick in Norse times; Sweyn Asleifsson had a strong family connection with Freswick.

Leaving aside the problem of Lambaborg, the three sites of Old Wick, Brough and Borve do form a group characterised by the placing of the great tower, in the two extant examples a plain square keep, to one side of the approach path. This contrasts with the late tower-houses of Girnigoe and Bucholie where the tower is a gatehouse. The most reasonable explanation of the group is that these castles are related to the Norse control of Caithness and Sutherland. There is sufficient reason to suppose that plain towers of the same type were being built in Orkney in the twelfth century and that some Scandinavian examples date from this period. The Lambaborg story suggests that the use of the Caithness promontories as sites for fortifications was not unfamiliar at the time. Borve Castle is of course named from Old Norse borg and this name's occurring in a very heavily Gaelicised region may indicate the age of the structure. Clearly, the castles form an historically interesting group which deserves much closer study.

Finally, mention may be made of an enigmatic structure on the isthmus of Lambhoga Head in Dunrossness, Shetland (fig. 28; National Grid reference HU 408140). There is a natural rift across the approach, and on the seaward side of this is a complex of structures built close up behind a bank or rampart. The most notable feature is a rectangular building of very fine-quality drystone masonry measuring internally 12.2 m x 6.7 m; the width especially is greater than that of a traditional Shetland croft house of the longhouse type. At the centre of the complex is an entrance gap flanked by massive boulders at each end of the passage. Extending back along the N edge of the promontory at right angles to the main building, is a subsidiary range which possibly comprised livestock pens. Lambhoga Head lies in a depopulated area which now is rough pasture and there is no local explanation nor any documentation. The structure could be mediaeval and is obviously defensive. The disposition of the main range of buildings across the approach is reminiscent of Sverresborg, but there are no dating indications; it is perhaps more likely to date from the late mediaeval or immediately post-mediaeval period. Without excavation it is impossible to relate it to the castle-building practices of either Scotland or Scandinavia.

BIBLIOGRAPHY

Admiralty, 1949, *North Sea Pilot Part 1*, 9th edn, London.

Anderson, J., 1893, "Notice of Dun Stron Duin, Bernera, Barra Head", *Proc. Soc. Antiqs. Scot.* 27, 1892-3, 341-6.

Anderson, J., 1901, "Notices of nine Brochs along the Caithness coast...excavated by Sir Francis Tress Barry", *Proc. Soc. Antiqs. Scot.* 35, 1900-01, 112-48.

Avery, M., Sutton, J. E. G., & Banks, J. W., 1967, "Rainsborough, Northants., England, Excavations 1961-5", *Proc. Prehist. Soc.* 33, 207-306.

Bernier, G., 1964, "Les Promontoires barrés des Iles Vannetaises du Mor Bras", *Annales de Bretagne* 42, 67-74.

Calder, C. S. T., 1939, "Excavations of Iron Age Dwellings on the Calf of Eday, Orkney", *Proc. Soc. Antiqs. Scot.* 68, 1938-9, 167-85.

Callander, J. G., & Grant, W. G., 1934, "The Broch of Midhowe, Rousay, Orkney", *Proc. Soc. Antiqs. Scot.* 68, 1933-4, 444-516.

Childe, V. G., 1935, *The Prehistory of Scotland*, London.

Childe, V. G., 1940, *Prehistoric Communities of the British Isles*, London and Edinburgh.

Clarke, D. V., 1970, "Bone Dice and the Scottish Iron Age", *Proc. Prehist. Soc.* 36, 214-32.

Clarke, D. V., 1971, "Small Finds in the Atlantic Province—Problems of Approach", *Scot. Arch. Forum* 3, 22-54.

Cleasby, R., & Vigfusson, G., 1874, *Icelandic-English Dictionary*, Oxford.

Clouston, J. S., 1931, *Early Norse Castles*, Kirkwall.

Clouston, J. S., 1932, *History of Orkney*, Kirkwall.

Clouston, J. S., 1936, "Three Norse Strongholds in Orkney", *Proc. Orkney Antiq. Soc.* 7, 1935-6, 57-74.

Cotton, M. A., 1959, "Cornish Cliff-Castles", *Proc. West Cornwall Field Club* 2, 1958-9, 113-21.

Cotton, M. A., 1961, "Relationships between Iron Age Earthworks in France and Britain", *Ogam* 13, 103-13.

Curle, A. O., 1946, "The Excavation of a 'Wag'...at Forse, Caithness", *Proc. Soc. Antiqs. Scot.* 80, 1945-6, 11-25.

Curwen, E. C., 1937, "Querns", *Antiquity* 11, 133-51.

Dietrichson, L., & Meyer, J., 1906, Monumenta Orcadica, Christiania.

Dryden, H., 1857, "Notice of the Burg of Mousa in Shetland", Proc. Soc. Antiqs. Scot. 3, 1857-60, 123-4.

Fischer, G., 1951, Norske Kongeborger I, Oslo.

Gordon, A. S. R., 1941, "Excavations of Gurnards Head...Cornwall", Arch. Jnl. 97, 1940-1, 96-111.

Hamilton, J. R. C., 1956, Excavations at Jarlshof Shetland, Edinburgh.

Hamilton, J. R. C., 1968, Excavations at Clickhimin Shetland, Edinburgh.

Harbison, P., 1971, "Wooden and Stone Chevaux-de-frise in Central and Western Europe", Proc. Prehist. Soc. 37, 195-225.

Hawkes, C. F. C., 1971, "Fence: Wall: Dump: From Troy to Hod", in Jesson & Hill (ed.) The Iron Age and its Hillforts: Papers presented to Sir Mortimer Wheeler, Southampton.

Jackson, K. H., 1964, The Oldest Irish Tradition: A Window on the Iron Age, Cambridge.

Jakobsen, J., 1936, Place Names of Shetland, London and Copenhagen.

Lamb, R. G., 1973, "Coastal Settlements of the North", Scot. Arch. Forum 5, 76-98.

Low, G., 1879, Tour through Orkney and Schetland in 1774, Kirkwall.

MacGibbon, D., & Ross, T., 1889, Castellated and Domestic Architecture of Scotland, vol. III, Edinburgh.

MacKie, E. W., 1965, "...Broch and Wheelhouse Building Cultures of the Scottish Iron Age", Proc. Prehist. Soc. 31, 93-146.

MacKie, E. W., 1969a, "Radiocarbon Dates and the Scottish Iron Age", Antiquity, 43, 15-26.

MacKie, E. W., 1969b, "The Historical Context of the Origin of the Brochs", Scot. Arch. Forum 1, 53-60.

MacKie, E. W., 1971, "Continuity in Iron Age Fort Building Traditions in Caithness", in Meldrum (ed.) The Dark Ages in the Highlands, 5-24, Inverness.

MacKie, E. W., 1974, Dun Mor Vaul: An Iron Age Broch on Tiree, Glasgow.

Mitchell, A., 1881, "Notice of...Hogsetter in Whalsay, Shetland", Proc. Soc. Antiqs. Scot. 15, 1880-1, 303-15.

Mooney, J., 1926, "Deerness: its Islands", Proc. Orkney Antiq. Soc. 4, 1925-6, 25-30.

Mowat, J., 1940, "Bucholie Castle", Old-Lore Miscellany of Orkney Shetland and Caithness, 10, 143-7.

Mowbray, C. L., 1936, "Excavation at the Ness of Burgi, Shetland", Proc. Soc. Antiqs. Scot. 70, 1935-6, 381-6.

Murray Threipland, L., 1943, "Excavations in Brittany 1939", Arch. Jnl. 100, 128-49.

O'Kelly, M. J., 1952, "Three Promontory Forts in Co. Cork", Proc. Royal Irish Academy 55, section C, 25-59.

Orkneyinga Saga, ed. Finnbogi Gudmundsson, Islenzk Fornrit vol. 34, Reykjavík, 1965.

Peacock, D. P. S., 1968, "A Petrological Study of Certain Iron Age Pottery from Western England", Proc. Prehist. Soc. 34, 414-26.

Petrie, G., 1890, "Notice of the Brochs or Large Round Towers of Orkney", Archaeologia Scotica 5 part 1, 71-94.

RCAMS, Royal Commission on the Ancient and Historical Monuments of Scotland, Edinburgh.

RCAMS 1911a Caithness (3rd Report, part 2).

RCAMS 1911b Sutherland (3rd Report, part 1).

RCAMS 1912 Wigtownshire (4th-5th Reports, vol. 1).

RCAMS 1914 Kirkcudbright (4th-5th Reports, vol. 2).

RCAMS 1946 Orkney and Shetland (12th Report: 3 vols.).

Scott, L., 1947, "The Problem of the Brochs", Proc. Prehist. Soc. 13, 1-36.

Scott, L., 1948, "Gallo-British Colonies: the Aisled Round-House Culture in the North", Proc. Prehist. Soc. 14, 46-125.

Simpson, W. D., "The Broch of Clickhimin", in Simpson (ed.) (First) Viking Congress, 19-45, Edinburgh.

Stevenson, R. B. K., 1955. "Pins and the Chronology of the Brochs", Proc. Prehist. Soc. 21, 282-94.

Stevenson, R. B. K., 1970. Review of Hamilton (1968). Antiq. Jnl. 50, 123-5.

Taylor, A. B., 1938, The Orkneyinga Saga, Edinburgh.

Watt, W. G. T., 1882, "Notice of the Broch known as Burwick or Borwick...", Proc. Soc. Antiqs. Scot. 16, 1881-2, 442-50.

Westropp, T. J., 1910, "Promontory Forts...in Co. Kerry", Jnl. Royal Soc. Antiqs. Ireland 40, 6-31, 99-131, 179-213, 265-96.

Wheeler, R. E. M., 1943, Maiden Castle Dorset London.

Wheeler, R. E. M., 1957, Hill Forts of Northern France London.

Williams, J., 1777, An Account of some remarkable Ancient Ruins lately discovered in the Highlands and Northern Parts of Scotland, Edinburgh.

Young, A., 1962, "Brochs and Duns", Proc. Soc. Antiqs. Scot. 95, 1961-2, 171-98.

INDEX

Aithbank 53, 86
Aithsetter, broch 82
Anderson, J. 1
Arbroath 1
Ardtreck, Dun 39, 40
Aywick (see Stoal)

Barra Head (Sron an Duin) 38-9
Barry, Sir Francis Tress 20, 74, 75
Belgae 60-1
Belle-Ile-en-Mer 54
Berwickshire 6
Beveridge, E. 4
Bigging, Brough of 20, 68, 77
Borgastoon, Brough of 52, 84
Borness Batteries 58, 59
Borve Castle 90-2, 95
Borwick, broch 20, 66, 77
Braebister, Brough of 34, 76
Brittany 6, 54, 59-62
Brough, Castle of 90, 91, 96
Bucholie Castle 90, 92, 95
Burgi Geos 26-33, 37, 39, 40, 41, 68, 69-70, 84
Burland, broch 34, 64, 82-3
Burraland, broch 34-5, 38-9, 70, 82
Burrier Head 83
Burwick, Castle of 53, 58, 76-7

Caesar, C Iulius 6, 59-60
Cahercarberymore 54, 59
Calder, C. S. T. 15
Calf of Eday 15
Camp du César 54
Carloway (Càrlobhagh), Dun 7
Carrigillihy 59
Celtic peoples 3, 6, 16-18, 41-2, 69
Channel Isles 54
chevaux-de-frise 27, 31-2, 40, 74
Childe, V. G. 4, 12, 60, 69
Chun Castle 2, 16
Chysauster 2
Clarke, D. V. 4, 61-2, 69

Clickhimin 3, 7, 11-19, 26, 29, 33-5, 37, 39-42, 64, 69
Colonsay 37
Cornwall 4, 16, 54, 58, 59, 62
Cotton, M. A. 54
Crosskirk (Caithness), broch 66
Cobbie Roo's Castle 94
Culswick, broch 1
Curle, A. O. 12, 25

Deerness, Brough of 6, 68, 79
dice 61
Doonabinnia 58
Doon Eask 54, 59
Doon Point 58
Dornaig (Dornadilla), Dun 2, 7
Dryden, Sir Henry 2
duck-stamped ware 60
Dun Mor Vaul 61

Eask, Doon 54, 59
Egils Saga 65, 88
Eilean nan Caorach 71

Faeroe 62
Flubersgerdie 37, 86
foot-marked stone 17
Forse, Wag of 39
Freswick 96

galleried duns 1, 2, 3, 38, 39, 70, 82
Galloway 6, 54, 58-62
Garth, Brough Ness of, 68-9, 83
Giants' Castle 58-9
Girnigoe, Castle 92, 96
Girston Bay 53, 76
Glastonbury 60
Gote o'Tram 68, 75
Graham, A. 3
Grugaig, Dun 39
guard-chambers 37-8, 61
Gurnards Head 54, 58-9
Gurness, broch 2, 65

Hamilton, J. R. C. 3,4,11-15,19-20, 19-20,35,40-1,69
Harbison, P. 31
Hebrides 2,4,38-40,43,53,60-1, 64,69-70
hillforts 1,6,37,61
Hog Island Sound 43-9,54,58,62,66, 68-9,83
Holborn Head 73
Houbie, broch 64
Huxter, Loch of 11,15-16,26,29, 33,35,37,39,40-2,69

Iberia 31
Iceland 62
Ile Istelec, Sauzon 59
invasions 3,13,16,16,41,66,69
Ireland 4,31,53-4,58-60

Jackson, K. H. 3,16
Jarlshof 3,4,11-13,39-41, 65

Keiss, broch 65
Kemps Walk 58
Kenidjack Castle (St Just in Penwith) 58-9
Kenmuir Graves 58
Kercaradec 54,59
Kervédan 54
Kirklaughlane 58
Kolbein Hruga 94
Krûn o' de Ora 86-7

Laing, S. 2
Lambaborg 96
Lambhoga Head 96
Landberg, The 43-9,54,58,66, 68-9,81-0
Lilleborg 92
Little Woodbury 2
Low, G. 76,81-2

MacKie, E. W. 1,4,37-40,61,69
Man, Isle of 6,31,54
Mhairtein, Dun 7,25-6,35,38,72
Midhowe, broch 2,11,18-20,26, 34-5,38, 64-5,69,80
Mitchell, A. 15
Mousa, broch 1,2,3,7,38,40,65, 68

murus duplex 38
murus gallicus 54

Neck of Brough 73
Ness, Broch of 20,74,96
Ness of Burgi 11-13,16-17,19-20,26, 33-7,40-2,64,81
Ness of Garth, Brough 68-9,83
Nether Bigging 78
North Fort of Scatness 26,33,35,42, 81
Nybster, broch 11,19,26,34-5,38-9, 70,75

Old Wick, Castle of 90,92,95
Onstan 53,78
oppida 59-60
Ordnance Survey 43,71,84
Orkneyinga Saga 65, 89
Oxtro, broch 65

peat 27
Pictish language 42
pins 61
place-names 42, 69
Portadoona 59
pottery 16,29,60-1,77,81,85

querns 61-2

Rainsborough 59
Richardson, J. S. 12
Riggan of Kami 26,33-4,37,39,42, 79
Ringill, Dun 39
rings 61
Rumps Point 58

sagas 65,88-9,94,96
St Johns Point 74
St Just in Penwith, Kenidjack Castle 3
Sand Geo, Castle of 68,78
Sauzon, Ile Istilec 59
Scatness North Fort 26,33,35,42,81
Scott, Sir Lindsay 2,3,4, 60-1,68
Scott, Sir Walter 12
Seanachaisteal 71
Semibrochs 4,38,40
Sgarbach 25-6,35,37,38,75
Simpson, W. D. 3,13,19, 66,70

Skirza Head, broch 20, 74
sling 50, 59-60
Snabroch 64
South Barrule 31
Sron an Duin 38-9
stepped ramparts 38, 59
Stevenson, R. B. K. 2, 18-19
Stoal, Brough of 7, 43, 50, 53, 54,
    58-9, 68-9, 84
Stronsay 68, 80
Sumburgh Head 11, 41, 80-1
Sumburgh Røst 41
Sverresborg 92, 96
Sweyn Asleifsson 96

Taing of Brough 37, 86
Telve, Dun 7
Trondheim 92

Uragaig, Dun 37

Vaul, Dun Mor 61
Veneti 6, 59-60
Virkie 41

Wainwright, F. T. 78, 88
Wales 4-5, 31, 54
Wessex 1, 37, 61-2, 69
Westropp, T. J. 54, 58
Wheeler, Sir Mortimer 58
wheelhouses 2, 3, 61, 65
Wigtownshire 58
Williams, J. 2
Windwick, Brough of 43, 50, 53-4
    58-9, 68-9, 77
Wirk, The 94

Young, A. 4

Pl. 1   Ness of Burgi after restoration in 1971

Pl. 2   Clickhimin, NE end and rear of blockhouse

Pl. 3   Loch of Huxter

Pl. 4 Dun Mhairtein, view down on fort from the higher cliff on the mainland side

Pl. 5 Dun Mhairtein, looking along isthmus towards ditch and rampart

Pl. 6   Burgi Geos from E

Pl. 7   Burgi Geos, view from the blockhouse back towards the land

Pl. 8   Burgi Geos, chevaux-de-frise and avenue, looking landwards

Pl. 9   Burgi Geos, the vertical cliff on which the blockhouse stands

Pl. 10 Burgi Geos, front face of blockhouse and enclosure wall

Pl. 11 Burgi Geos, ringwall to rear of blockhouse

Pl. 12 Scatness North Fort, looking S over outer bank

Pl. 13 Scatness North Fort, E end wall-face of blockhouse exposed at cliff edge

Pl. 14 The Landberg, from NNW

Pl. 15 The Landberg, looking across horseshoe-plan bank towards main rampart at crest of slope

Pl. 16 The Landberg, outer banks viewed from main rampart

Pl. 17 Hog Island Sound, outer banks from N

Pl. 18 Brough of Stoal, looking across geo from NW

Pl. 19 Brough of Stoal, outer slope of middle rampart

Pl. 20 Castle of Sand Geo

Pl. 21 Brough Ness of Garth, view from hillside looking NW

Pl. 22 Brough Ness of Garth, the middle terrace-wall

Pl. 23.   Castle of Old Wick from W.

Pl. 24.   Castle of Old Wick, great tower and ditch from SE.

Pl. 25.   Borve Castle from SW.

Pl. 26.   Castle of Brough from SE.

www.ingramcontent.com/pod-product-compliance
Lightning Source LLC
Chambersburg PA
CBHW041705290426
44108CB00027B/2864